KOKODA - THE TRACK BACK

KOKODA - the Track Back

RUTH JAMES

Allied Learning

First published in Australia in 2023
by Allied Learning ABN 39 529 683 360
alliedlearningonline@gmail.com
Copyright © Ruth James 2023
All rights reserved.
The right of Ruth James to be identified as the author of this work has been asserted under the *Copyright Amendment (Moral Rights) Act 2000.* This work is copyrighted. Apart from any use as permitted under the Copyright Act 1968, no part of this book may be reproduced, copied, scanned, stored in a retrieval system, recorded, or transmitted, in any form or by any means, without the prior written permission of the publisher. The author has made every effort to contact copyright holders for the use of material in this book. Anyone overlooked who requires acknowledgement should contact the author.
All paper product in this publication is provided by environmentally responsible certified mills.
Cataloguing-in-Publication data is available
from the National Library of Australia :
https://catalogue.nla.gov.au/
James, Ruth (Author)
Kokoda - the Track Back
ISBN: 978 0 6454539 3 5
Front cover design by Canva
Front cover image of Ruth and John on the Kokoda Track near Deniki
by Len Stanford
From personal collection:
Rear cover image of Edevu Primary School students on Parade 2018
Rear cover insert of Efogi class students 2017
Spine image of Kokoda Track arches, Kokoda.
The dedication page Kokoda Primary School image is from personal collection.
Illustrations: 2013 - Len Stanford, Ruth James
Illustrations: 2015 - Cliff James and Ruth James
Illustrations: Efogi, 2017 - Ruth James
Illustrations Edevu, 2018 - Ruth James
Illustrations - KTF, 2019 - Clyde Arabata, Ruth James, KTF
Illustrations - Carriers: Saii Faoli, Philip Laba, AWM013993; Sam Geseng, AWM306818; Maryanne Suma, Evelyn Jarua, AWM100457; AWM100459.

DEDICATED TO THE ENDURING TEACHERS OF
THE LEGENDARY KOKODA TRACK AND
ITS REMOTE PROVINCES.

Kokoda Primary School, Kokoda Track.
Papua New Guinea 2019
Photograph from personal collection

Contents

Photo Insert vi
Introduction ix

1	Anzac Day Tour - Kokoda 2013	1
2	Anzac Day Tour - Kokoda 2015	41
3	Efogi 2017	71
4	Edevu 2018	99
5	Kokoda Track Foundation Research Project 2019	135
6	Kokoda Track Foundation's Origins and Programs	161
7	Legacies of the Carriers	167

Somewhere Along The Kokoda Track 197
About The Author 199
Afterword 201
Acknowledgements 203
Farewell 204

Introduction

The unthinkable of July 1942 was suddenly real. Japanese troops had landed at Buna and Sanananda and were headed this way along Papua New Guinea's peaceful heart - the *Kokoda Track*.

With our defences laid bare; our troops fighting in the European theatre of World War 2; Australia's collective hopes fell on the shoulders of a detachment of young, inexperienced part-time soldiers, untrained, untested and under the gun. Aware that reinforcements would not arrive from the Middle East for several weeks, the 39th Battalion held out heroically until the late August arrival of the 2/14th Battalion in the final hour at Isurava. Their baptism of fire had written Australia's underestimated sons into history, acknowledging their distinction as seasoned soldiers to fight as equals alongside their battle-hardened reinforcements.

But more butchery was coming...*much* more...almost the entire length of the Track as our Australian troops leapfrogged in strategic withdrawals back to Imita Ridge. By now, the Japanese were wreckage themselves. Starving, unequipped and with their supply lines targeted for Allied bombing raids, they found themselves retreating and subsequently ejected from this South Pacific island nation.

As much as this constitutes the *heavy lifting* of the Papua New Guinea Campaign, heavy lifting came in another form; a kind, attentive, seemingly inexhaustible form known so affectionately as the *Fuzzy Wuzzy Angels*. Without them, Australia may not be enjoying the freedoms shared today.

Countless powerful shoulders, four to each stretcher, carried the maimed and dying through dense and treacherous terrain to Medical Stations positioned along the Track. Reportedly, the native carriers were as gentle as nurses, providing care and assistance to the wounded, ever-watchful and ready through all conditions. These same shoulders carried supplies and equipment, built shelters, loaded and unloaded stores, cleared jungle areas, buried the dead and later exhumed the bodies for reinterring at Bomana War Cemetery, Port Moresby.

Crucial in navigating, the Fuzzy Wuzzies were World War 2 guides, a role their sons and grandchildren uphold today, continuing their legacy as professionally commissioned porters.

Having experienced these quiet and caring souls in action along the Kokoda Track, I similarly envisage their naturally attentive forefathers with the wounded. Their swift reflexes, sure-footedness and agility are beyond our typical abilities, as proficient as many of us believe we are, but then we are talking about the Kokoda Track. This is their home.

Over ten years since my first Anzac Day trek paying homage along the jungle track, I still cannot explain why this brutal endurance run has left its indelible effect on me. A trek is a trek is a trek, right? For some of us…no. Its magnetism reaches deep and steers you into a place within yourself you didn't know exists. It is the very reason I return repeatedly to tackle the beast and, further yet, to teach its remote children English, a dream that was born the moment I saw them in 2013.

The Kokoda Track changes many trekkers spiritually, others cannot wait to go home, while the rest purely test themselves against its might, and I have trekked with all three. For me, its spectral lure is inescapable.

And so, with one more life changed, the dream commenced.

* * *

Chapter 1

Anzac Day Tour - Kokoda 2013

> KOKODA - OWERS CORNER (24 April to 4 May 2013)

There are times in your life when quests cannot wait any longer, and for me, this was one of those times. I was on a mission. It was a case of *Keep up or step aside.*

Haunting me for years with its subtle taunt, the Kokoda Track had woven itself into my life like a call waiting to be answered. Some would ask *Why,* while others knew me well enough not to ask at all, which was probably just as well, for not even I knew the answer. Does anyone when it comes to the legendary Kokoda Track?

It is simply enough that it *is.*

BRISBANE - PORT MORESBY (24 APRIL 2013)

Occasionally, I dared break away from my contented reading to check the Air Niugini flight's progress as we neared the tropical coast of Papua New Guinea's Southern Region. Below, several islands dotted with palm trees were beginning to edge slowly into view, and I could see the Papuan mainland; in fact, I couldn't tear my eyes away from it.

It is 24 April 2013, and I am travelling solo, utterly absorbed in my plans for the next nine days, slogging it out on the inhospitable Kokoda Track. Quite a few trekkers on board evidently belong to various trekking parties, having prepared for one of the most enduring experiences anyone can voluntarily, or otherwise, put themselves through. Some will begin their compelling journey to walk from Owers Corner in the footsteps of our heroic Diggers, while the rest of us will fly to Kokoda village and make the long haul back to Owers Corner. This is known as the *Reverse Trip* or the *Reverse Traverse*.

Before long, scenes of terminal buildings and airport hangars were sweeping past as our plane's squealing tyres touched down at Port Moresby's Jackson International Airport. Within an hour of navigating Customs and retrieving my pack, I assembled with five other members of my group before Saii Faole, our welcoming representative of South Sea Horizons, shuttled us away to the Gateway Motel, which I'm told is owned by the Papua New Guinea Prime Minister, the Hon. Peter O'Neill.

Tonight sees me bunking with Aimee, a young Airlie Beach pharmacist who is also a well-travelled and seasoned adventurer, organised, resourceful and prepared for anything. Our spectacular view from our hotel room consists of the opposite wall and the hotel's cat prowling the industrial bins below, whereas the panorama from the lifts out to the Owen Stanley Range is positively stunning. I could stand there all day just looking at them.

Surprisingly, we are on Queensland time which somehow makes me feel like I haven't left Queensland at all, but my texts verify I am definitely in Papua New Guinea, and they are getting through to home just fine.

Returning downstairs for drinks with the others and a briefing in the function room, we were entertained by Papuan dancers in grass skirts dancing to bamboo pipe drums expertly beaten with rubber thongs, the tribal sound and the drummer's swift movements commanding absolute attention.

News reached us that a female trekker who was supposed to join us had to return home after the airport lost *all* her gear, pack, boots…everything. There was no alternative but for her to turn back. After enduring this volume of preparation and the endless checking and re-checking to ensure everything is packed, her utter disappointment must be excruciating. It renders my recent chaotic dream of leaving my boots behind suddenly insignificant, although still vivid.

More trekkers arrived on the late flight and were put up in a different hotel; no one really knows where except that they were a fair distance away. We are all meeting at the Anzac Day Dawn Service at Bomana War Cemetery tomorrow morning, so will gravitate together eventually.

Apprised by another South Sea Horizons representative of tomorrow's Dawn Service agenda and travel plans, a hotel guide accompanied us to KMC Kentmanica Fried Chicken…almost like your typical KFC back home, only the KMC here is protected by large bars, similar to those of a jail. The chicken was the same, though, and always, *always* better with coleslaw. We shouted our guide a meal and a drink which he enjoyed with us, the bars serving as a reminder that you don't go anywhere in Port Moresby without a guide, especially at night.

Plenty of laughs later, we understood each other a little more. Two of the older guys, Len Stanford and Peter Miller, were interested to know what book I had been reading a few seats up from them, as they noticed I barely looked up throughout the entire flight. When I told them it was *Kokoda Spirit* by Patrick Lindsay, they smiled knowingly and nodded.

Eventually, our group made the short walk back to the Gateway for last hot showers and comfortable beds before our nine days up the Track....no more waiting!

PORT MORESBY - KOKODA - HOI (25 APRIL 2013)

Meeting in the downstairs Reception at 4:30 am, we were fully kitted to trek on the conclusion of this extraordinary Dawn Service. It was Anzac Day, and ours was the second of two parties leaving for Bomana War Cemetery, waiting till nearly 5:20 am before discovering there was no bus coming back for us. Finally, the bus was urgently summoned, and we arrived in perfect timing for the start of the service; we'd just received our crash course in *island time*.

Bomana War Cemetery; I have never experienced anywhere so surreal. The Owen Stanleys make a violent backdrop for the 3,824 graves here, including the 699 belonging to unknown Commonwealth soldiers. For a place bearing such torrid history, it has an unrivalled beauty.

In the coolness of the breaking dawn, Australia's Governor General Quentin Bryce, PNG's Prime Minister Peter O'Neil, and several other dignitaries took turns delivering their amplified speeches to the silent crowd gathered before them. The only movement was the PNG and Australian flags as they stirred gently in the morning freshness.

Then, it came. Those haunting notes of the bugler's *Last Post* filled the silence, followed immediately by Papua New Guinea and Australia's national anthems. To listen to the Papuan's singing their captivating anthem is to be transported. There is a magic in their harmonising that affects you with every lilting note.

As the growing light illuminated the thousands of marble headstones, a distant low thumping could be heard from the direction of the Owen Stanleys. Stealthily and surely, the Blackhawk helicopters flew in low formation, growing ever closer on the approach for their breathtaking fly-over. By now, the light had increased enough for some relatively clear photos, or at least I hope they turn out alright.

The trip back to the motel was an adventure in itself. We were stuck in a traffic jam for what felt like forever, and our plane was supposed to leave at 8:30 am. The first lot of dignitaries, Prime Minister O'Neill and our Governor General sped past under police escort with sirens blaring, their national flags flying from their diplomatic cars.

About 15 minutes later, the second lot of dignitaries went through, also under escort, so our driver pulled out after them joining the motorcade to much cheering from our bunch. This must have taken a solid hour off our agonising wait.

Accompanying us on our return to the Gateway Hotel was a party who had trekked to Kokoda and flown back to Port Moresby yesterday afternoon. One of these guys, now in his 40s, had walked the reverse trip from Kokoda a couple of years earlier, returning to walk the Track from Owers Corner. This was it for him. He struggled more this time and wouldn't be doing it again in a hurry.

We were welcomed back to the hotel with a sausage sizzle breakfast before retrieving our gear for loading onto our waiting bus. Heading to the airport was an education in itself, though. Australian road rules evaporated before our amused eyes as we followed utes and trucks overloaded with passengers hanging on any way they could for a free ride.

Finally, we boarded *Tropic Air Cessna PS 20H* for Kokoda. Well, most of us...Len Stanford, Peter M. and John G. remained behind for the plane's return as we'd reached the maximum weight limit. Kokoda's airfield remains the grass airstrip it was back in 1942, mowed with a slasher by the locals. An unexpected greeting awaited us as dozens of inconvenienced eagles flew off lazily while we landed, returning to their foraging once the plane had taxied to a stop.

Ironically, on its return to Port Moresby, news came of the plane breaking down, requiring a further 2-hour wait for repairs; not the most encouraging sign. Concern gradually paralleled with awe as I took in this almost mythical place at the foot of its dominating mountains, and I couldn't believe I was here.

My thongs seem to have either vaporised in my big pack or I have left them in the car back in Brisbane (At least they weren't my boots, as envisioned in my dream.), so our guide, Barnabas Omi, escorted me to the local market to buy a pair for PNG K16 (16 Kina). The shop has the same bars as KMC, so business as usual.

Betel Nut juice is everywhere you walk, a sight easily mistaken for blood at first look. Betel Nut, colloquially known as *buatau* or, more simply, *buaie*, is the green palm nut chewed for its high. The red-stained mouth and teeth from the nut's residue mixed with lime are tell-tale signs of its consumption, a unique consequence of this national pastime.

Three hours later, on Len, Peter and John's safe arrival, we left for Isurava but only after our lunch of noodles, Spam, cheese and Salada biscuits. Aimee suggested sprinkling some grass on our lunch for greens, followed immediately by Len's thoughts on Spam, which amused everyone no end; *The taste of Spam is indescribable.*

Once issued with our packs of lollies and nut bars for the Track and utensils rinsed, we left through the symbolic Kokoda Track Arches in the steady rain, Kokoda's ultimate send-off. The pristine village of Kovelo just outside of Kokoda is the prettiest little village I've ever seen; neat, palms everywhere and just the sweetest little place behind a curtain of rain. And from there, it rained full-on the entire way to Hoi, where we have stopped for the night. The walk so far has been relatively flat, passing a substantial coffee plantation mid-way.

Joining innumerable patriots throughout the decades, I visualised Australian and Japanese troops advancing in single file along this muddy track and looked for bullet marks in the trees. Here at Hoi, some of the trees look possibly scarred by bullets, yet couldn't be 70 years old. Aside from this, the war-torn Kokoda Track of 1942 would be vastly different from today's revered Track, although there are signs if you know where to look. I don't, but there you go.

The boys happily kicked back in the creek alongside our campsite at Hoi once we arrived. Len, Peter, Geoff, Russell and John G. immersed themselves in the rocky creek for some sheer relaxation, taking in the solitary atmosphere.

After a dinner of Spaghetti Bolognese, Barnabas and the guys sang to us in the most perfectly harmonised voices I have ever heard. My porter is 22-year-old Ladiva, very kind and around my height, so a *shortie*. He makes sure I have enough water and refills my water bottle from the nearby creeks, where I drag my Aquatabs from their specific place in my day pack to purify the water by the time I need it. These gurgling creeks run with inviting, crystal-clear water, easily mistaken as pristine, while villagers upstream are washing clothes and bathing, so purifying tablets are crucial.

Aimee and I are up the far end of an open-frame long hut, and our clothes won't dry because, of course, it's raining, but what a beautiful sound. And the water rushing over the rocks nearby brings the most serene peace; a wild peace.

On 25 November 2013, seven months after our Cessna 208B Grand Caravan delivered us, amid engine trouble, to the legendary Kokoda Airfield, the single-engine craft lost power at 9,000 ft and was guided into an attempted forced landing at Western Province's disused Kibeni Airstrip.

Tragically, the resulting crash became a recovery mission for three of the ten onboard, their bodies retrieved from the partially submerged wreckage on the banks of the Palbuna River.

HOI - ALOLA (26 APRIL 2013)

Breakfast of cereal and coffee was organised by these fantastic porters. Their headlamps bobbed as they moved around in the dark, setting the fire to boil water for coffee and washing up before breaking camp at 6:30 am. Our lead guy, John, explained that no one must go out in front of him, and although I've trained hard in the past months, Aimee and at least five others are seriously fit young athletes, so John takes them ahead of us.

Len, Peter, Russell and I are all fairly middle-aged, ranging from 48 to 62, with Geoff and Graydon being father and son, the pair who were the late arrivals. Graydon turns 21 during this journey and stays with his dad and their porters, Obar and Elijah. Aimee refuses to allow her porter to carry her heavy pack but lets him take her smaller one instead. She is a powerhouse and competes in a 10 km marathon on Hamilton Island a couple of days after returning home.

These were the first steep climbs, the first up to Deniki, an indication of what is yet to come, but not too slushy. Isurava was coming up, last night's intended destination that we couldn't make following our late departure from engine failure. I bailed on lunch at Isurava Village, as I couldn't stomach Spam two days in a row...to be fair, it's probably tinned corned beef, but I just had nut bars instead.

It was a steep descent to Isurava Memorial. Located in the most incredibly surreal spot, about 20 minutes outside the village, nothing can prepare you for its impact.

The granite pillars displaying the etched words *COURAGE*, *MATESHIP*, *ENDURANCE* and *SACRIFICE* cast their own power against the vast backdrop of the Kokoda Valley, once ringing with relentless gunfire raining death. It was here, accompanied by Papuan Infantry Battalion combatants and enveloped by some of nature's harshest terrain, that Australia's stalwart Army Reserves of the 39th Battalion, the originally underestimated Militia unfairly referred to as 'chokkos' (chocolate soldiers that would melt in the heat of battle), blazed and slayed resiliently into history to save Australia from invasion. It was almost a forlorn hope that reinforcements, the seasoned 2/14th Battalion, would make it in time. Thankfully, they did; another hour could have been too late.

Bruce Kingsbury's fearlessness changed everything here. Remembered in history's annals for mercilessly hosing the Japanese with unrelenting machine gun fire, Kingsbury mowed down wave after wave of attacking Japanese from his position on a boulder, galvanising the Australian troops to hold fast. His Victoria Cross was awarded to him posthumously, a sniper's bullet having sealed the fate of this gallant 24-year-old as he stood on his now-memorialised Kingsbury's Rock.

Photos at the Rock were relatively leisurely until the rain came over the mountains and, with it, our cue to leave. Instantly the Track became sticky and terribly difficult. True enough, you can almost set your watch to the rain coming in around 2:00 pm every afternoon. Onwards and upwards to John's *Let's rock and roll up!*

Massive climbs, *immensely* steep, awaited us on the way to Alola. Surely, I can't be the only one who can't get Eric Clapton's song, *Lola*, out of their head, although this rendition now assumes some of my own lyrics. Well, it does take my mind off skidding uncontrollably onto my ass in the mud; three more busters today. Eventually, we came around the last corner to the stunning view of the perfect little village of Alola nestled against the backdrop of the Owen Stanleys - it took my breath away. This unforgettable scene will stay with me always.

The one distinctive obstacle separating us from where we stood and washing in the waterfall at the edge of the village was the steep descent we faced, every step threatening another potential disaster. Arriving into camp 45 pensive minutes later, we knew where we were heading - straight to that tumbling water for a much-anticipated wash. The creek eddies through the rock pool before cascading over the rock face before us, a natural infinity pool. Alola's enchantment is literally something else.

Dinner tonight was mashed potato with bits of meat and onion in it, my instant favourite, which really hit the spot. I showed John, our lead guy, my *Kokoda Spirit* book, and I was astonished when he identified Barnabas in one of the photos. Of course, Barnabas was immediately handed my pen, to the astounded man's delight.

There were more surprises as John discovered his uncle and niece in a couple of the photos, as well as other porters who weren't in our party, so I had him sign their photos, too, before leaving the book with him to enjoy the sentiment a bit longer. The porters are so friendly, kind and gentle, and it is a pleasure being among them. They sing to us in their own language, in those exquisite harmonising tones, and to hear it moves me. The sound is mesmerising.

There is a storm out in Oberi Valley tonight. Clouds have rolled through below us, shrouding the bottom of the mountains to leave the ragged peaks looming like shadows in the deepening dusk.

This is the most beautiful place on earth.

ALOLA - TEMPLETONS CROSSING (27 APRIL 2013)

Coffee and protein bars are proving to be the ideal breakfast for managing these hefty climbs, especially bars studded with chocolate, as cereal leaves me wishing to bring up the heaviness in my stomach. The body works in mysterious ways, so we'll see what changes along the way. I have also discovered the importance of unloading any excess 'luggage' from your system. It is a wonderful thing just how well the body responds to that one simple function, and conveniently, so far, so good.

We left Alola behind us at 6:20 am after a night of hammering rain, so the steep descent was particularly treacherous. Ladiva shadows me, holding onto my pack for my own stability during these rugged stretches, his swift reflexes having saved me from countless disasters.

This morning's jaunt was yet another measure of their agility in this brutal terrain, like their Fuzzy Wuzzy Angel forefathers and ancestors before them. Many don't wear shoes. Instead, the strong toes on their broad feet curl to grip the slick terrain, shoring their footing masterfully with each step.

Making it to Templetons Crossing by mid-morning, we discovered its spectacular arched bridge was, in fact, a memorial in itself. John explained the fighting and battle positions held here during the Japanese retreat. The Aussies had a seriously high vantage point, almost encircling the starving Japs before forcing their retreat towards Alola. One look at those surrounding mountains and the advantage was clear. The Aussies had it squarely over them.

John G., 61, really struggled today and fair enough, too; it was one *long*, sapping haul. We stopped between Templetons Crossings 1 and 2 for a lunch of noodles, peanuts, corned beef and cheese. Ian Kero, our cook, is amazing. He's the last to leave camp after breakfast, loading himself up with his pans, utensils and supplies to jog past everyone, wherever we are, before bowling on ahead to pitch camp in preparation for a hot lunch on our arrival. He's really something else.

One of the younger guys, Peter, miraculously kicked over an old rifle cartridge case as he was walking, entirely unexpected and a gift as it happened. Not there for the history, he didn't want the precious, corroding shell, so offered it to Graydon's dad, Geoff. It came to light in that moment that this trip means a great deal to Geoff, his late father having fought here in 1942. He is leaving some of his dad's ashes at Ower's Corner after taking him back over the Track one last time as a family, their lives touched forever; grandfather, father and son.

Templetons Crossing 2 is the whopping Eora Creek, noisy *and* beautiful, where I washed my clothes in the rushing water as it started to rain. It was 2:30ish, and the thick, drenching rain just fell straight down. I can't believe this incredible place.

Too brisk to swim, I braved letting the chilly water massage my feet until they were numb. I didn't care less, I just needed to soak them. So far, I don't have any blisters having taped my toes and any hot spots every morning and rubbed Bepanthen into them at night. It is the difference.

We arrived here at around 2:10 pm, a good 8-hour hike and very slippery. I know when it's about to get tough as Ladiva positions himself, ready to help me. Hiking sticks are invaluable, halving the effort of lifting your body weight; I wouldn't do this trek without them.

All bleating aside, it is phenomenal what our soldiers endured. Their perseverance through dysentery and scrub itch while suffering every other disease and injury, all while being shot at, is hard to imagine; unfathomable horror in such a breathtaking place. And then, as if the sheer magnificence isn't enough, the beauty of tonight's full moon is devastating. I have never seen anything like it.

TEMPLETONS CROSSING - DIGGERS CAMP (28 APRIL 2013)

We've now split off into our two groups; Gekkos, the party's go-getters, comprising Del, Aimee, Tim, Greg and Peter, who continue on to Owers Corner in the next four days, leaving Len, Peter M., Russell, Geoff, Graydon, John G. and myself, just the seven of our hearty rabble-rousers.

After topping PNG's highest peak, Mt Bellamy, John, our Lead Guy, helped me carve my initials into an immense fallen tree marking the summit. Climbing this landmark demanded adherence, pushing us to dig deep on reserves and slog on in the footsteps of our Diggers while imagining gunfire throughout the mountainside. Experiencing the increasing intensity of this brutal place has made its remote wilderness a part of me, and as much as I will be sorry when this journey is over, I know its power will shadow me.

Geoff and John G. are toughing it out and are never far behind us, and their porters help them every step of the way. It is a monstrous effort. I've managed to knock skin off everywhere, including a gash on my right shin when I skidded in two directions on some rocks...that hurt.

Ian had a hot lunch waiting for us at Camp 1900, so named as it is 1900 ft above sea level, a beautiful little place with welcoming native huts and thatched rooves...serene and peaceful. Then onto the crash site of the Beaufort Bomber, which has been picked apart for scrap metal over the past 70 years.

John told me the villagers had tried excavating the wreckage, but the idea was abandoned when the hole quickly filled with water, the site being left as a memorial instead.

Leaving for Diggers Camp shortly after, we found a dead cuscus, also known as a *vauri* in PNG's Motu language. And, of course, the unfortunate marsupial became quite the subject. Ladiva said to Ian *Dinner's ready* and everyone simply cracked up. John was over at the edge of the clearing waiting for us and didn't know what was going on. He has the fierce expression of a warrior but welcoming with a gentle heart.

We arrived at Digger's Camp within half an hour and were greeted by the most picturesque vision of a gentle stream bordering those beautiful, neat native huts with their backdrop of ancient Pandanus; I had no idea they could grow so tall; some must be 25-30 metres! I just sat out in the rain for nearly an hour absorbing it all, as I won't be able to once I get back home. I've already decided I'm coming back.

Chris, Russell's porter, came out to make sure I was alright, and during the conversation, he told me he was hoping to finish high school in the next couple of years. He left school early to work along the Track, just one of the thousands fighting for whatever opportunity they can in a place terribly restricted for choices, yet remaining hopeful.

After eventually drying off and changing, I made my way over to the long hut where the Boys had a fire going, and we all sat around talking with John, Barnabas and some of the others. Obar, Geoff's porter, had particularly bad feet from blisters (not used to his shoes evidently), so Geoff put ointment on them, assisted further by Gray offering him a pair of socks.

Tea tonight was Spaghetti Bolognese, a little different but hitting the spot regardless, and before long, the porters were singing for us. There is one particular Papuan song that lingers with me, and three particular words stand out; *guba guba* and *bena abia,* but that's all I know.

Surprisingly, I don't feel tired or sore, and my muscles are fine, the whole purpose of preparing well. The jungle noises can be shrill sometimes, too, particularly when the night cicada peals like a buzz saw through the dark.

Gentle rain is falling right now, although I'm sure it's bound to get heavier. I just love it here.

Guba guba is Motu for skies or storms; bena is then; abia is to get/take. The song is shared in blessing.

DIGGERS CAMP - EFOGI (29 APRIL 2013)

Straight out of camp at 7:00 am into the jaws of unforgiving steep climbs just about did us all in. The one reprieve breaking our mental and physical anguish was our arrival at Naduri to meet one of the few surviving Fuzzy Wuzzy Angels, who I'm told is 110 years old, but don't quote me on that.

We waited for a short while until his doors were opened for us, and there he was, sitting in a wheelchair with the PNG and Australian flags behind him. His name is Ovuru Nidiki, and taking my book up onto his porch with him, I asked if he would sign his 2-page photo, a happy image of him waving to the camera. Compassion suddenly became overwhelming as it occurred to me that perhaps he couldn't even *see* his photograph. Ovuru found it difficult to write as he appears to have had a stroke and is quite frail, but the kind man still managed.

Others from my party went up to shake his hand and thanked him for his committed service to our troops in the suffering of 1942. John took my book again for safeguarding, and when I glanced back, Ovuru was looking directly at me. For a moment, his eyes peered directly into my soul to such a depth it haunts me. Perhaps he could just see me more clearly, but either way, I won't ever forget those gentle, dark eyes.

It seems *what goes down must come up* along the Kokoda Track, and we were soon moving on to face the toughest stretch so far, the brutal descent to Efogi Creek ahead of an equally harrowing climb. Efogi Creek rushes beneath your precarious steps across the log bridge while an iron grip holds onto your pack, ensuring you only stay saturated with sweat.

This was the perfect water stop, our short break, before scaling the waterfall's steep rockface to the small village of Launanumu, otherwise known as Efogi 2. This was where the Kokoda Track had toyed with me long enough.

After all my relentless training, ruthlessly preparing for anything this brutal experience could deal me, the exhausting clamber to Efogi walked me to a standstill two-thirds of the way up. Ladiva stepped off the path, positioning himself dangerously to help me, half dragging me up the treacherous, taunting mountainside.

The Japanese carried lanterns through the night here, a scene that filled the Australians with awe as hundreds of flickering lights brought death to them, the site destined for one of the most ferocious battles to take Efogi. That said, the Australians had the high ground, heaping grenades down on the Japanese climbing the near-vertical slopes like proverbial mountain goats.

I didn't trust my judgement when the mountainside eased into that gradual curve of the last few metres, but the punishment *was* finally over. This was Launanumu. Too smashed to stop in the rain at the monument, we bought bananas on our way past the stalls of fruit and drinks and came to a welcome standstill at the lunch hut. Noodles, tinned tuna, peanuts, Sao biscuits, and cheese never tasted so good!

Efogi, the historic village and our camp for the night, waited for us just down the hill about 20 minutes away, but that didn't matter in our relief. Anything purchased helps the locals, so we dug into our pockets in the meantime.

A considerable village of roughly 400 villagers, Efogi is the big brother to Launanumu, but you don't see many people here. The name Efogi will forever remind me of exhaustion and merciless climbing, and I don't know how these gentle people in these remote highlands of Papua New Guinea cope with this terrain. Clearly, they're born to it, no question.

This is Barnabas Omi's village, where his brother is chief, so Barnabas will stay with his family tonight. He showed us around Efogi and explained some of their Highland culture. Apparently, a dowry for a wife can be one cow, and for amusement, Geoff asked him how many cows I would be worth; *two* according to Barnabas. So now I'm affectionately known as *Two Cows*; quite the honour...I think.

We were shown our digs, where we gratefully unloaded our wet gear and chose our four-person rooms in a high-set long hut overlooking the museum and our mess hut. Len, Peter and I are bunking together, and our wet gear is draped on every available nail, rail, and hook. The only dry clothes I possess are the ones I sleep in, but we occasionally manage to dry our clothes over the fire, which I am presently attempting.

Peter's air bed punctured back at Templetons Crossing and deflates within an hour, so he's struggling to sleep, although I hardly imagine anyone's getting their regular beauty sleep just now. I've come to the conclusion you have to drop a Panadol at night to take the edge off. It works for me.

What also works for me is the cosey warmth of tonight's glowing fire...and this popcorn!!

EFOGI – MANARI (30 APRIL 2013)

Before we broke camp, the museum was opened for viewing the rusted weapons and artifacts recovered throughout the neighbouring slopes. Not only were the walls lined with guns, artillery and grenades, but a samurai sword, tin hats and the remains of boots, one of which still had bones in it. It wasn't pretty, but the experience lingers.

We were already packed and ready to go, so when we'd finished at 7:00 am, we made our way through Efogi to pick up the Track, passing between the hospital on our left and the short Efogi Airstrip a little further along on our right.

The sight of such a short airfield instantly generated reluctance to be any unfortunate pilot landing a plane here, despite being considered the campaign's holy grail, particularly during the Japanese occupation. They, too, witnessed these stunning views across the valley to Launanumu in the misty mornings, only this was not why they were here.

Once again, after carefully negotiating the rugged descent to another creek crossing, we braced ourselves for the inevitable uphill jaunt, although not as harsh as yesterday. Protein bars and lollies for breakfast still work, but a bucket of coffee would go well. Coffee sachets are *essential* and duly noted...better make that doubles!

There was a clearing at the top where we stopped briefly, and what we saw when we turned around was a sight I will never forget; Efogi spread out before us. The surrounding hills, blue in their own shadows, were shrouded in clouds, making the village's lush green plateau even more dazzling. Suddenly, the strain of the climb disappeared.

After ten captivated minutes, we set off around the bend, carved from the mountainside with its jagged rockface on one side and breathtaking drop on the other, climbing on until we finally reached Brigade Hill. John had explained that the Japanese had advanced along Mission Ridge below us to our right on their way up to Brigade Hill, where they ambushed the Australian troops, inflicting serious casualties.

Ahead of us, as we stepped out of the jungle and into the clearing, was a small monument adorned with wreaths and petals between two flags; one Papua New Guinean and the other Australian. But that was not the only significance. Four rows of 16 sticks, each row equally spaced and around 3 metres apart, were carefully and deliberately positioned, almost as if they were sentries. And why?

Each of these sticks represents every Australian who died in the battle for Brigade Hill, their bodies left unburied by the Japanese when they took the high ground in their push towards Port Moresby. Only after some weeks, the Australians returned following the retreating Japanese.

Bivouacking in the dark, surrounded by the stench of death, they woke at dawn to find their dead mates around them. Finally, they would be laid to rest there on Brigade Hill overlooking the beautiful valley below until their time came to be exhumed and their remains re-interred in consecrated ground at Bomana War Cemetery. And so, now, these carefully placed sticks on this remote hill in the most unforgiving terrain represent each man, a silent reminder to us all of their endurance, courage, mateship and sacrifice.

In our hushed preoccupation, we attempted to comprehend the brutality of the battle that took place beneath our feet, the lives lost so we could even be here paying homage, and feeling inadequate because we cannot fathom their torment.

To the right of the Track, in a thatched open hut, some villagers were selling their bananas at the usual price of PNG K5 (approx. AUD $2.50). Wherever you buy them here, they are the sweetest and most delicious bananas you will ever taste, probably due to the rainfall, and we have an ongoing arrangement; one of us will buy a bunch to share between us.

Eventually moving on, we found hiking comparatively easy, still with its fair share of tricky stretches and disasters, but thankfully, nothing drastic. For the first time, I didn't have any major busters myself.

In the gloom at the base of a rotting tree is a carved-out knarl where the last remaining Japanese soldier from his company hid as the Japanese withdrew. It is believed this same soldier returned many years later to find the remains of his fallen comrades and take them home as he had promised their ever-present ghosts.

Len explained to me that this man, Kokichi Nishimura, wrote a book called *The Bone Man of Kokoda,* and he found it a particularly interesting read. His tree stands to the left of a shadowy foxhole dug by the Australians, now mostly filled from 70 years of rain, mud and leaf litter falling into its depths.

At this stage, John and some of the porters have come down with cold symptoms, some worse than others. Some have also been suffering badly from blisters, and it seems likely that trekkers have kindly given them shoes that don't fit the porters properly, so they suffer for it. They must also have some form of first aid, but trekkers provide them with plasters and anything else they need. We all carry lollies (M&Ms mainly because they melt in your mouth, not in your hand!) for energy boosts, sharing them gratefully with our porters. It is the least we can do right now.

Russ, Peter, Len and I stopped outside of Manari at a lush boulder-strewn catchment to wait for the others to catch up. We'd crossed the Vabiavu, the river spanned by yet another native bridge of two fallen logs and a rope. It's a treat to watch the porters crossing them so effortlessly; they could sleepwalk across without falling in! I'm guessing they must wonder how we even manage to walk at all without help.

Eventually, continuing on to Manari, 40 minutes away, we climbed what felt like forever until emerging into the heat and open field of Kunai Grass. The Track soon led us past flourishing cornfields bordered by log rails, the airstrip and Manari School on the outskirts of the Village.

By sheer chance, a Ulysses, the national butterfly, bright blue and black with its swallowtail, was hovering elusively between patches of pink flowers alongside the track, where I finally managed a photo of it.

Manari kids are so happy and kind to each other, and the first thing we saw when we arrived at our hut was the vine swing where they played, giggling with infectious laughter as we stood watching them enjoying themselves. I had a go on it with them, and I haven't laughed so much for so long!! I gave them all some party face masks and lollies, and they loved them, something I've been doing for the kids in every village where we've stayed. I would dearly love to come back and teach English to the kids along the Track one day, and every step compels me even more.

At this point, I was happily anticipating an enjoyable lazy afternoon relaxing with everyone and couldn't believe it when I discovered we actually have luxuriously soft mats and pillows! It was as if we'd just been ushered into the Ritz; I felt so spoilt. My immediate thought was of gratitude to the beautiful people of Manari for making us so welcome as I happily claimed my corner where my packs fill the extra space.

After lunch, we met another Fuzzy Wuzzy Angel, a real character who let me take his photos. I'm told he's 97 or 98 years old, but he's at least in his 80s, the cheery Faole Bokoi.

Weighing down his shirt were medals of all kinds. Australian military badges, Police Guard and Papuan badges honoured his service, but almost out of view under the brim of his Australian Slouch Hat was the Rising Sun badge, ready to pin the left side up into place. He was joined by a kind lady I can only presume is his wife, whose eyes carried a tenderness that told me so much about her. My photo of this timeless couple together captures the moment perfectly, and I promised to return with copies for them when I can.

Many of the porters' families live here, so they will stay in their own homes tonight. John and the rest of the porters are staying in the neighbouring hut, and later in the evening, Manari's school children, ranging from very young to high school age, came to sing for us - the sweetest thing.

I discovered later that Faole Bokoi is the father of my South Sea Horizon's trip coordinator, Saii Faole, back in Port Moresby, and the sweet lady with the kind eyes is, in fact, his mother, Ovela Hotoki.

Her home was originally Diggers Camp, where I sat contentedly in the rain for an hour, wishing I didn't have to leave.

MANARI - NAURO (01 MAY 2013)

Last night's sleep was perhaps the most peaceful any of us have had so far. Len has taken to flickering his headlamp on the ceiling in the morning as our wake-up system. He's such good value, they all are, and we've all essentially become good, like-minded mates.

Right on schedule at 7:00 am, we left Manari to begin our mammoth climb to Ladavi Saddle, followed by another serious descent with one horrendously steep section. This time, it was more of *What goes up must come down.*

And then the mud...*actual,* real mud everywhere for miles!!! It's not as though there was anything new about the mud, just its overwhelming volume.

We had to walk around its perimeter at every opportunity because to walk in it, your boots just get stuck in this gooey, slurpy clay-like mud for about five sludgy kilometres. And logs!! Whatever you do, don't slip off the logs, or you'll fall on your battered-enough butt into the stinking mire or slip down between two of them, and that's not what you need either. It's the Brown River swamp, hot, with its suffocating, insect-laden air. No wonder it's considered evil by the population!

Alternatively, nothing teases your senses more or beats that reviving vision of a gurgling, shallow creek when you are covered in sweat and mud from head to boots, and exertion gives way to playful relief in the rejuvenating waters. While we recovered, John and Ian swiftly knocked up this fabulous little table out of bamboo in no time at all, tying the structure together with vines so neatly it was pretty to watch. And then lunch was ready. These guys truly are the champions their grandfathers were.

Heading off again an hour later, we crossed the Brown River (not brown, just not clear), and I was surprised to see a few conveniently fallen trees to cross...with a little help. This was supposed to be one of the crossings we were to wade across, except the river was too high after the consistent storms. The water still came halfway up our calves as we crossed, but miraculously my feet stayed dry in my gortex-lined Lowa Renegades, a worthy investment.

As it happens, Russ and I are the only two without blisters, the rest suffering from them since getting their boots wet at the crossing. Their struggles continued until finally, after one more steep climb, we reached the pretty little village of Nauro, its neatness as positively captivating as Alola's. The two are my favourite places along the Track. And the village has a shower, so I washed my hair for the first time since Port Moresby; that makes it seven days...the pleasure was more than you can know. I was so hot and sticky, and the water so cold that it left me with head freeze.

Washing some clothes was the next luxury, and *then* I actually felt quite human. But I do love this beautiful place overlooking Nauro Valley. Clouds are rolling in, and distant thunder reverberates in the hills around us, typical mid-afternoon timing. This whole place is absorbing me into its world. I feel it.

It is no surprise to have come down with the cold going through the whole gang, so Geoff kindly gave me some Ibuprofen. We've all gone to bed ready for tomorrow's early start, to the porters singing in the night around their campfire, and no words can do the sound justice. I don't want to leave.

NAURO - UAULE (02 MAY 2013)

Sunrise at 5:00 am was stunning.

Mountain peaks silently dominated the clouds in the early light as if indirectly listening to the porters singing to the morning, its magic defying all description in one of my life's rarest moments. All I can say is I drank my coffee s-l-o-w-l-y, leaning against the corner post of the mess hut, desperately wanting to stay but knowing I had to go.

There was no warm-up tackling Maguli Ridge. It was unapologetically rugged - too rugged - starting directly at the edge of our campsite. There is no good time for a head cold, and today was no exception, especially after only 30 minutes of sleep. Sniffling miserably with every step, I battled on until finally making it to our water stop halfway up the ridge, where I got stuck into the lollies and chocolate, boosting my energy levels no end. Russ also gave me a couple of Glucodin, that simple addition to my effervescent electrolyte tablets; I don't know how I overlooked it.

Once again, I was fuelled, unstoppable and ready to face the slope's worst challenges until reaching the top, where the boys began singing their most stirring song so far. The words were in their native language, and everyone simply stopped talking, turning our heads toward them to listen. I don't know what we listened to, but we'd never heard anything like it.

The rest of the day couldn't have been in starker contrast, the terrain being immeasurably easier and mostly downhill. Partway down Maguli Ridge was a section called *Japs Ladder*, which sounds as chilling as it is; the site of the Japanese equivalent to our Diggers' long-gone *Golden Staircase* on the other side of Imita Ridge. We finally reached the Japanese zigzag trenches at Ioribaiwa, in all their haunting presence. They are largely silted up now, leaving them only about 300mm deep, but the sight of them chills the blood to visualise Japanese soldiers in their positions right at our feet, intent on decimating our Diggers at all costs.

We continued on through picturesque Ioribaiwa Village, stopping to pay our respects at the memorial dedicated in English and Pidgin. This was where the Australian troops fought tooth and nail before tactically withdrawing to Imita Ridge, including the 2/25th Battalion, the unit of Pte Roger Percy Cambell Stedman QX3169, my great aunt's then fiance.

This wasn't his first rodeo. His battalion had been recalled from the Middle East to reinforce the battle-weary 39th and 2/14th, but no one was prepared for what awaited them on their arrival at Templetons Crossing; mutilated mates and fellow Diggers, their cannibalised body parts contents in pots around the deserted camp. Tormenting sights like these hover like ghosts, forever unseeable.

Now, in the shadow of their fate, we continued on to Uaule, making a number of inviting creek crossings that systematically filled my boots with water. It was around here that Ladiva pin-pointed a toucan high in the jungle canopy. I tried to take photos of it, but the mid-sized bird blended too darkly with the foliage surrounding it. It seemed black and white with a hooked beak, but hopefully, I'll get a better chance another time. Ladiva is also looking out for a Bird of Paradise for me as we hear their characteristic calls all around us but can never see them. If I have it right, I think they're called *Manuti* in Ladiva and John's individual language, although not Pidgin.

The crossings were enchanting, here, swathed in ferns and lush vegetation with the same stream twisting and bubbling its way across the track numerous times. The Japanese didn't make it this far, 48 hours from Port Moresby, but they'd seen the city's searchlights in the night sky and naturally believed they were as good as there. Thankfully, that wasn't to be.

Instead, with supply lines destroyed and zero reinforcements, the starving Japanese were given the order at Ioribaiwa to turn 180 degrees and walk on (*retreat* not recognised in their vocabulary) under a cloak of humiliation, crucifying any shred of remaining faith.

Unsurprisingly some of us hit that brick wall today ourselves. Pete, Graydon, Geoff and John G. all took about 11 hours to finally arrive at camp. Len and I took around 8 hours, and Russ came in about half an hour after us.

We all enjoyed a therapeutic swim down at the river as we came into camp, our second splash today. We'd waded through another creek crossing at lunchtime, where we discarded our packs and literally fell in boots and all, which was just what we needed in the growing heat having come down from the highlands. By now, it didn't matter; you just swim for its sheer relief and everything else goes away.

Shoulder massages go a long way on these punishing slogs, assisting the porters, especially under their enormous loads, so I spent a little time just freeing up their painful shoulders. The massages evidently worked, providing great relief with better flexibility afterwards. Some suffer from shoulder injuries sustained from football, with NRL being their passion. Wouldn't you know it, most of them support Queensland in the State of Origin, and the Brisbane Broncos is their favourite team! Now, that's what I like to see.

After we were settled in for the evening, I asked everyone to sign my book on the inside cover, including anyone who was in the book itself. It is my honour and privilege that they share their lives with us in one of the most difficult terrains on earth so we can experience this journey.

Ultimately, there are those among us, porters included, with some very sore feet covered in blisters. Thankfully, I've persevered with plasters on the hotspots of my feet every morning to prevent blisters, and it has been the difference. I have avoided them, which demonstrates the importance of spending those few minutes in the morning to prepare your feet. And largely due to that simple fact, I actually feel good, considering we've slogged nearly 90 km.

There are some things I will definitely take away with me for future trips:

1. Coffee bags - don't leave home without them.
2. Lollies - Fuel up at the bottom of a climb and charge on.
3. Salt / Glucodin – I needed salt after each harrowing climb and Glucodin to assist the electrolyte tablets.
4. Bepanthen - always rub it into your feet at night.
5. Lightly scented moisturiser - it's luxurious.
6. Sleeping - stow this cherished, dry attire in a waterproof bag like its gold.
7. Panadol - one before bed, and sleep will come.

UAULE - OWERS CORNER (03 MAY 2013)

We were supposed to leave in two groups an hour apart this morning, so no one could have been more surprised than Len, Russell, Peter and I when we received expectant looks from John as we lounged in doorways and on stairs.

Hurriedly grabbing our packs and throwing our boots on, we were gathered with the others within minutes and, soon after, were crossing the same river eight times, which was nice.

Then came Imita Ridge, your meanest nightmare and equally as memorable. It just about did me in.

Believed to be the original site of the *Golden Staircase* with its 3,000 log stairs, Imita Ridge was the stronghold where the Australian soldiers dug in, waiting for the final advance of the Japanese. Hauling that 25-pounder gun up this sheer slope is unimaginable when you've actually seen the terrain. However they accomplished it, those heroes made a miracle happen.

The Japanese, in the meantime, had exhausted their capacity. Having begun their retreat, they encountered the embittered Australian forces later at Templetons Crossing, where they were mercilessly thrashed all the way back to where they had originally landed at Buna and Sanananda. The successful ploy had stretched the Japanese too thin. Job done.

Today, I reached the belief I couldn't handle much more of this uphill stuff, but thankfully, the climbing was virtually over, and it was all downhill after this labyrinth we presently faced. Tree roots washed from infinite downpours and eroded with equally as many boots, acted as footholds all the way up the Ridge, then the same again all the way down the other side. And the mud; *yeah, good on it*; sticky, clay-like mud, until we reached the Goldie River, where I followed Ladiva into the rushing, stony water. Of course, I fell in, pack and all. Great, really, because it was stinking hot, and we were all saturated with sweat. I was hopelessly amused and couldn't stop laughing. John and Ladiva were worried at first until they saw the funny side themselves and started laughing, too.

Panic surfaced about half an hour later as Geoff hadn't come in yet, so John and Wilson headed up the track to look for them. Within 15-20 minutes, John was carrying him across the river, then holding him upright to get him up the bank.

Seeing the struggle, I came down to support Geoff from the other side. He was a mess, dehydrated and full of blisters, so I got a hydration tablet into him and kept cool cloths on his head and neck to cool him down. Laying in the shade of the hut with a wet cloth over his eyes finally revitalised him, and he was ready to have some lunch.

Struggling to support him along the way, Obar, Geoff's porter, was worse for wear himself, so I gave him a hydration tablet, too, while Graydon put powder on his feet to help with his burst blisters. The Kokoda Track will have its pound of flesh.

Eventually, we were back in our boots, walking on alternating level ground and gentle downhill grades lined with ferns and boulders before stopping for a short break. Ahead of us was our final climb to the arches of Owers Corner. Strangely, though, our porters suddenly seemed to disappear, but there is always a guaranteed reason.

So in safe resignation, our conversation turned to the slab of SP Lager, the gang's beer of choice, that Barnabas was known to have organised with Saii over the satellite phone back at Imita Ridge in readiness for our arrival. We'd unanimously agreed to shout our porters beer and pizzas later tonight, an offer that brought beaming, enthusiastic smiles from each of them. We are all positively starving for both.

These gentle souls, descendants of the beloved Fuzzy Wuzzy Angels, are kind-hearted, polite, and some of the most respectful people I have ever met. When it comes to our debt of gratitude for the life-saving service their fathers and grandfathers, uncles and great uncles provided us during the battles along the Kokoda Track, dig deep. For battles fought by the Royal Papuan Constabulary along the entire length of the Kokoda Track, through to the northern beaches of Buna, Gona, Sanananda and beyond, yes, perhaps dig a little deeper. Make no mistake, we would not be here if it weren't for them; they are why we can be.

Our porters returned, and to our complete astonishment, they had made us the most beautiful headdresses of hibiscus and foliage back at Goldie River, presenting them to us with the greatest joy on their faces. Keeping them hidden must have been a task in itself, and I won't ever forget their happiness at that moment. It is a moment that will always make me smile.

Then we set off for the last time. The lush jungle rainforest, green and shadowy, surrounded us until we broke from its cover to face our final climb to Owers Corner. You don't stop, you keep going and going until you see the tops of the timber arches. And then we were finally there.

I was the first through our magnificent finishing point to find Saii and his boys with our carton of cold SP as promised; it couldn't have been more perfect. The exhilarating sense of achievement was weirdly laced with finality and grief, and as I gazed out over the Owen Stanley's, its intensity become all the more breathtaking. During this quiet reflection, Geoff buried his father's ashes, complete with the old rifle shell, in an emotional family goodbye accompanied by Graydon. Nothing seals memories or bonds stronger than the heart.

We all took photos, and as I took my last one, the battery in my camera went flat – perfectly timed as I was done. I sat on the top step overlooking the terrain where the 96 km Track lay concealed, and although we had made it, its sheer intimidating ruggedness made our feat difficult to believe. To face the Track for the first time from this end with its geographically longer climbs would be to face the jaws of hell itself.

There was a storm rumbling in the distance as if in begrudging farewell or daring the next trekking party, I can't decide which, and Ladiva came and sat with me. We told stories about our families, and I discovered he'd lost some family members in the tsunami back in 1998. He also likes curries, chicken and fish, and I told him about my uncle and aunt, who lived in Lae and Kundiawa for 12 years until 1967. I also told him that Barnabas is going to find out if it will be alright for me to teach English at Efogi School for a couple of weeks when I can get the opportunity to come back and teach one day. It may take a while, though.

With everyone keen for hot showers, Saii's mini-bus took us all back to the Gateway Motel where, around 6:00 pm, we met up with our porters one last time. Our evening of beer and pizzas included watching the NRL, our own National Rugby League, with my Brisbane Broncos losing 12 - 26 to the Rabbitohs, if you don't mind. It didn't dampen my spirits, though.

More wonderful surprises awaited when our porters presented us with gifts. Ladiva gave me a beautiful string bag known as a bilum, woven with beige, purple and green threads made from bark – it is truly beautiful. His sister made it, and I plan to hang it in my spare room where I can see it every day when I walk past.

Each of us gave our porters some money, although Len and Peter considered giving their boots to their porters, also. They'd washed the boots off as best they could but decided they were unlikely to get through customs at the airport. I was definitely keeping mine for my next trip up the Track, though.

As it was, one of the Gateway staff kindly offered to wash mine off and have them back to me dried in time to pack them later tonight. I discovered all too late that drying them meant he would be putting them through a commercial dryer. I would suggest waterproofed Lowa Renegade military boots with a Gortex membrane are not meant to go through commercial dryers! That said, I smiled as I thanked him for his generous efforts and gave him PNG K5. Lesson learnt.

Del from our original group was here, too, and joined us, sharing his stories of gruelling 11 – 12 hour days to finish in eight. Incredibly, he'd had keyhole knee surgery six weeks earlier, so it was a grind for him. He's fine, though, and flies home tomorrow.

I charged my phone and sent a text home, my first contact with family or the outside world in nine days. But for all my eagerness to see my family at home, again, I will miss the early dawns in the Owen Stanley's shrouded in clouds and the porters' beautiful singing. This raw wilderness, the people, the dream to teach here and this deep shift within have deeply affected me.

You can leave the Track, but the Track won't ever leave you.

Roger Stedman would return in 1945, but he and Elsie were not destined to marry. Elsie remained unmarried until her death in 1977.

* * *

Black Hawk fly-over during Anzac Day Dawn Service,
Bomana War Cemetery 2013.

Isurava War Memorial 2013.

Our ill-fated Tropicair Cessna at the Kokoda Airfield 2013.

Templetons Crossing Camp 2013.

Templetons Crossing area 2013.

Templetons Crossing area 1942.
Photograph courtesy of the Australian War Memorial.

Efogi hut 2013.

Overlooking Efogi on the way to Brigade Hill 2013.

(From left to right) Geoff, Graydon, Len, Peter and Russell at Naduri 2013.

Ovuru Ndiki, one of the last Fuzzy Wuzzy Angels, Naduri 2013.

The Ulysses, PNG's national butterfly. Manari 2013.

Faole Bokoi and his wife, Ovela Hotoki, Manari 2013.

Tobin Saky (middle), one of the children playing at Manari's swing 2013.

Crossing the Brown River between Manari and Nauro 2013.

The remains of a zig-zag trench near Ioribaiwa 2013.

(From left to right) Ladiva, unknown, unknown, Len Stanford, Graydon, Ruth, Russell, John (leader), Wilson and Wesley at Owers Corner 2013.

Chapter 2

Anzac Day Tour - Kokoda 2015

> KOKODA - OWERS CORNER (24 April to 4 May 2015)

Cliff, the eldest of my three brothers, ten years older than I am and not to be outdone by his little sister, was determined to accompany me on my second trek from Kokoda to Owers Corner, regardless of my initial objections.

It would be a repeat of my first trip, only with a difference - this pivotal experience would live on between us.

Essentially, the Kokoda Track is my compass; just mine; but sharing five months of training and preparation was a good leveller, developing ourselves as a team and understanding this diverse side of *us*.

Our planning involved many phone calls across 360 km of South East Queensland; Cliff in Brisbane, and me in Bundaberg. Training also brought its competition as we crowed about our tough climbs in nearby national parks, Cliff's being Boonah and Mt Cotton, and mine, Mt Walsh, Mt Woowoonga and the Bunya Mountains where I had trained previously.

Interestingly, it was during these months I encountered my first and only echidna in the wild as I laboured up Mt Woowoonga. It was the scuffling in the leaf litter that naturally drew my attention to find the spiny critter waddling unconcerned and not the snake I envisaged, after all.

In stark, unsettling contrast, returning down that same mountain after a triple training hike, my momentum took me through an Orb Spider's web, its host at head height silhouetted strikingly against the spreading sunset. The vision I have of myself is that of a dog uncontrollably chasing its tail as I tried desperately to unhitch my pack while keeping an eye on the spider, no doubt equally as surprised as I was, and moving ever closer to my head! Amusing now but not so much then.

Although Cliff indirectly trained by walking upstairs regularly in his everyday life, I took that exercise a little further by pushing myself frequently through 1,250 step-ups as well as running 5 km most days, both routines seeing me through last time and would again now.

And before we knew it, the day had arrived.

BRISBANE - PORT MORESBY (24 April 2015)

Two years ago today, right to the timing, I was preoccupied at the Brisbane Airport jostling the same Black Wolf backpack and tan Oztrail day pack, both containing almost identical contents today as they did then. The only significant difference was the company; a silver-haired big brother just waiting to be dragged through the mud!

Plenty of empty seats surrounded us on our Virgin flight, so while David Attenborough captivated my attention, Cliff slept in an adjacent aisle seat with more legroom. And he slept until we were descending over the same palm-dotted islands that I'd spotted on my earlier trip, with the same buildings and 1942 bunkers whipping past as we came into land at Jackson Airport at 1 pm. In the distance beyond the tarmac's boiling mirage, the defiant Owen Stanley Range generated that same primal sensation in me, as if I had no business daring to trespass within its rugged isolation. The unforgettable thundering power from those rolling storms reverberating through the valleys still reached into me.

Customs had relocated for reconstruction, redirecting our path through this orderly rabbit warren adorned with posters promoting the four-yearly Asia-Pacific Games being held in Port Moresby on 4 July. An exciting event for the Pacific region's countries, this year's games double as a magnet for Papua New Guinea's tourism, similar to Anzac Day. Evidence of this was the familiar sight of trekkers staggered throughout the collecting travellers, a picture that raised my curiosity...*How many have returned for the same reason?*

Collecting our packs from the rotunda, Cliff and I were met at the immense automatic doors by Saii Faole, who happily remembered me, to my pleasant surprise. I was reluctant to interrupt this kind man as he checked through his manifest, reminiscing shortly after until our remaining party of South Sea Horizons-Geckos trekkers located us. We were here, and so were the storm clouds gathering in the distance over those untameable mountains towards Sogeri.

Our waiting Holiday Inn Express shuttle was soon scrambling its way strategically through congested roundabouts and passing Digicel billboards before delivering us safely to the hotel's modern foyer, where we were soon checked in and settled into our rooms. Nothing is more recognisable than a group of newly returned trekkers looking forward to beer and pizzas following their arduous journey over the Track, and so it was that such a group was milling at the bar to place their orders when our party arrived for our briefing. Waiting at the tables were their porters, dependable and stoic, most having been on the trip with me two years ago...including John, Ladiva and Elijah, who were taken entirely by surprise. Their faces lit up like lanterns when they recognised me, and warm hugs swiftly followed. They had no idea I was returning. Great moments just get better, and John and Ladiva sat with us, catching up briefly before rejoining the others hungrily reaching for the closest of numerous steaming pizzas.

Our briefing was a great opportunity to get to know the others better, and a 75-year-old Canadian woman, Margaret, who barely looks any older than Cliff (not that he's *old*...just saying), is answering the Track's challenge. Adventure is her plaything, kayaking through the Arctic for one, so I look forward to hearing more stories in the coming days. Other greats who will be trekking with us include Kathy, Michael, Tash, Angus and Naomi, although there are more; I just can't remember all their names. Tomorrow's arrangements are to meet in the downstairs lobby at 4:00 am for breakfast before loading our packs onto the minibus and heading to the Dawn Service.

Presently, at 7:45 pm, we're all organised; final hot showers, alarms set, and now, the last soft beds for the next nine bone-cracking days await.

PORT MORESBY - DENIKI (ANZAC DAY 25 April 2015)

It was a 3:45 am start with a packed breakfast of sandwiches and fruit supplied by the Holiday Inn to fuel our morning as the bus grappled with Anzac Day's pre-dawn gridlock.

With packs stowed in the back, our arrival at Bomana War Cemetery was met with the sight of glowing candles dotting the gloom filled with an increasing crowd of patriotic locals and Australians. I caught up briefly with John again, and he is staying in Port Moresby to rest, so I wished him well and suggested perhaps he and Ladiva could meet up with us for pizza on our return.

Regrettably, there was no Blackhawk helicopter fly-over giving the Dawn Service that haunting undertone as the headstones illuminated in the brightening light, although the Owen Stanleys glowering in the distance more than made up for it. Victor Kirkwood, Cliff's best mate from school, had given Cliff the location of his second cousin's grave to pay our respects. Cpl. Cecil Mervyn Pikett had died from burns received while unloading fuel in 1944, but there was just no opportunity to find his resting place as our flight to Kokoda was waiting.

This time, Kokoda Museum was open to us, and we absorbed the artifacts retrieved from the area, as well as enjoyed the chance to wander around the three memorials dedicated to the Australian, Papua New Guinean and Japanese fallen.

There hadn't been any option to enjoy it on my last trip when Len and Peter's plane had broken down at Port Moresby; we'd had to wait for their party to arrive rather than wandering off. That is except for this 48-year-old blonde who needed to buy a pair of thongs at the local shop, thinking I'd left them behind in Brisbane. Interestingly, I had another exasperating dream of forgetting my boots, utter panic I can do without.

Back in today's trip, we regrouped for our porters to be assigned to us, and mine is Newton, a kind 41-year-old Port Moresby man, and Cliff's is Chris, our well-informed historian. James is great to talk with and very helpful also. He comes from Efogi, and his wife and nine-week-old baby wait for him there, so I'm sure he'll be glad to be home when we finally arrive.

And then, with introductions and preparations over, we headed off, following the road over the Kumusi River, where I made a point of walking through the first pothole I encountered, representing the inevitable ahead of us. When someone asked me why, my joyous answer was simply: *You'll see.*

Other members of our group are Andrew, Anthony and his son, Rick. Barnabas is even here with Obar, Geoff's porter from my last trip, although both are accompanying this trek's Gekkos group. Barnabas is as wonderful as ever, and I caught up with him for a while. He told me he had shown his kids the *Kokoda Spirit* book I sent him containing his picture, and they couldn't believe their astonished eyes, just as his couldn't the moment he'd seen it. Images of their shocked faces instantly filled my mind bringing my own unrestrained smiles.

We talked about the possibility of my teaching the kids English at Efogi, and he definitely thinks it can be arranged and encourages it. We agreed that once I've arranged my *TESOL* qualification, I'll organise the trip through Saii. Barnabas will be splitting off from us with the Gekkos group further along the Track, so none of my old mates will be here after that. Nonetheless, unpredictable exploits and unforgettable memories will doubtlessly unfold along the way.

At this point, we had lunch on the outskirts of Kokoda near the arches, and right on cue, it began raining steadily as if heralding our departure and the gruelling journey ahead of us. Experience prepared me for taking those photos I'd missed of Kovelo when I couldn't reach my camera, and of course, the village is as pretty as ever. Over in the distance, I could see the local villagers sheltering from the rain, waving and calling to us as we trudged past while others making their way from Hoi to Kokoda welcomed us with smiles and shy *Hello*s.

The steady rain soon increased to a solid downpour, accompanying us until our arrival at Hoi for a brief stop. Cliff is taking in the whole exhilarating experience, mud and all, just as I imagined. The pretty little crossing at Hoi brought back memories of Len, Peter and Geoff daring the chilly water for a swim and refresh. This time, though, after our break, we continued hiking up to Deniki where we have camped for the night. Chris explained to us that when our Australian soldiers were attacked here in the early morning hours, some hadn't even had the chance to put their boots on before returning fire and disappearing into the night to regroup and establish their positions. 1942 for our Diggers, those fathers, husbands, sons and brothers who fought here, is beyond our limited imaginations, as hard as we try.

After our dinner of Spaghetti Bolognese, the guys sang to us in that same stirring harmony that has been handed down through countless generations, singing from their hearts. The beauty of these mountains is doing it to me again; it's ethereal.

DENIKI - ALOLA (26 April 2015)

The worst caffeine-deprived headache plagued me through the night after all, resulting in very little sleep, but a good day still unfolded. We paced it out steadily, and it seems easier than last time, considering my nervousness about insufficient training. I've concluded that this nervous energy is *respect*; if you don't feel it, then you're treating the Track too cheaply.

So far, I haven't had any sore muscles or blisters but am dealing with a little chaffing today. I know I have Soov somewhere in my kit, but like so many things, I can never find it when I want it. So instead of Soov, I've used Bepanthen, which I'm again using on my feet at night, and wouldn't do the trek without it; it's the best thing.

Around lunchtime, one of the local residents presented a stimulating talk at Isurava Village, preparing us for our arrival at the stunning memorial, where we also stopped for lunch. This familiar track is absorbing me all over again into that same primal peace, that wild peace where nothing can reach you.

Lunch of noodles, tuna, cheese, peanuts and Saos may not sound particularly appetising but was eagerly welcomed by our ravenous party. An hour or so later, with the rain barely holding off, we'd packed up and were soon on the Track again for Alola. It is just the prettiest region, almost like the path between Uaule and Owers Corner, laced with delicate ferns and moss on either side, all sustained by streams and waterfalls. Neglected memories of just how gorgeous it is here returned abruptly, not only of the Track but overlooking the valley cradling pretty Alola Village, where we will camp once again.

Cliff is doing well and plans to stretch tonight. We had a swim at the waterfall and washed our clothes just by swimming in them, but jeez, it was cold! Big Brother then decided to have a camp down while I played a ball game with the kids, some being fascinated by my long blonde hair, giggling as they played inquisitively with it.

Overall, it was a fun time, and the kids loved the presents I gave them; more masks, coloured pencils and typical school stationery. One of the teachers explained that the school is back up the hill beyond the crest, so the kids have quite a haul every day just to go to school unless that changes one day.

Camped in a hammock beneath our hut was a middle-aged Alola man, escaping the heat of the PNG sun, although I can't say it was particularly hot. It remained fairly clear and sunny until late afternoon when storm clouds rolled in with a long peel of thunder, proving his chosen place perfectly ideal.

The clothes didn't dry at all, and I am quite chaffed now. I tried Pricky Heat Powder, Vaseline and Paw Paw Ointment, all unsuccessfully, so Tash suggested long pants, which made all the difference. I don't know how it works, but it did; the woman is a genius.

After tonight's badly needed Curried Chicken, Barnabas and I talked at length about Myola, where we will be heading on our way to Mikoko, a new village. Myola is where the supplies were airdropped for the troops along the Track, so we're looking forward to seeing this crucial point in our Boys' history.

Tragically, in a twist of woeful irony, some were accidentally killed by air drops landing on them.

What a gorgeous night here. The storm is rumbling out in the valley, and somewhere nearby, someone (possibly a porter belonging to another trekking party) is playing the guitar and singing outside one of the bamboo guest huts. He's having the best time and sounds so relaxed. Tonight, his singing and the soothing effects of Panadol will ease me to sleep.

Panadol, one of those essentials to get you through!

ALOLA – MIKOKO (27 April 2015)

We left Alola right on 6:30 am after breakfast, consisting for me of a muesli bar, the old favourite Smarties and a coffee lolly. Otherwise, it's really only cereal and Sao biscuits, not something I can deal with.

I'd forgotten there was a brief downhill walk, then the inevitable uphill stint, which was easier than I remember, funnily enough. Last night's chaffing was literally gone by morning and gave me no more trouble.

Huge amounts of uphill grinds kept us busy until our arrival at Templetons Crossing 2 for lunch, my opportunity to immerse myself in the camp's aura once again.

Cliff slogged it out bravely, but this morning's struggle was no surprise. He may find tomorrow easier if he feeds up on lollies; I know it works for me. This was where Gekkos split off from our party last time, but these guys will leave us at Nauro.

Templetons and Nauro are both special places with special memories among many, although Templetons is especially notable for me for another reason. This is where the full moon magically illuminated the jungle, and the noise of the creek rushing over the rocks filled the night. It is also where the last two lines of a poem formed in my mind...and stayed:

It's a place to fulfil a lifetime dream and feel your spirit change, Somewhere along the Kokoda Track in the Owen Stanley Range.

One day I'll write the rest of it.

All too soon, we were leaving Templetons Crossing behind for Mikoko Village, the new camp where we are currently surrounded by clouds. We're not quite halfway yet, but I've found this trek much easier, and Newton is superb, always there ready and such a kind man. Quite often, he will be helping Kathy simultaneously, as Thomas, our Lead Man and Kathy's designated porter, is generally ahead of her and out of reach.

That said, Kathy is impressively sure-footed and nimble, an astonishing feat in this terrain. Speaking of porters, Barnabas informed me today that both John and Ladiva are now commissioned as professional porters, so no surprises there.

We all sluiced off under a black poly water pipe bringing water into the village from the creek flowing down the mountain, and everything seems to be going to plan after all our training. It really is about recovery as much as endurance, proven by neither of us suffering from sore muscles. And my favourite tea on the Track tonight; mashed potato with bits of meat and some onion (I think) through it. As an alternative, this potato was served with pasta and was equally as amazing. Carbs on carbs, yes, for sure, but we're ravenous for whatever we can get!

Tonight's fire is in the long hut where we had tea, and Cliff, being the old Boy Scout he is, just loved stoking the embers with more firewood. Unfortunately for him, the wood he used was a little damp, resulting in two things; smoking us out *and* providing us with the unmissable opportunity to sledge him, much to everyone's amusement, including his. He loved it, and we had the best evening just kicking back. We might even get our clothes dry over Cliff's smoky fire, *and* they'll smell better!

MIKOKO - EFOGI (28 April 2015)

Early nights are followed by early starts; up at 5:30 am, breakfast at 6:00 am and out of camp at 6:30 am. This morning, out in the misty rain, Mt Bellamy waited. Decaying where it lay, the fallen tree marking the peak was still there, but my initials carved into the bark which had long since rotted away, were nowhere to be seen.

Cliff and I joined some of the others deviating to Myola with its vast grassy area straddled by small creeks and light swamps while the others made their way to Diggers Camp, where we would meet them later.

It was great to see the old 1942 landing strip this time, the view enhanced by clearer skies. From our lookout over the extinct volcanic crater, we could take in the geography coveted by both the Australians and Japanese, another revered driver for fierce fighting. A decidedly easier track than we'd been negotiating, too.

On our way to Diggers Camp, I slipped backwards between some tree roots and was stuck there like a turtle. I couldn't stand up or roll over, so I just sat there semi-reclined as if all I needed was a Smirnoff and the next anticipated NRL game. Kathy tried to lift me from a deadweight, but Newton came to the rescue lifting me back onto my feet with one hand. Cliff tried sledging me, but I just asked him how my footprints were looking from all that far behind, drawing amused chuckles along the line. A little mud and duress should not get in the way of some good-hearted humour.

We rejoined the others at Diggers, the home of Saii Faole's mother, Ovela Hotoki, instantly sparking my senses at the sight of this mystical place with those spectacular pandanuses overlooking the camp. Then on to Naduri, the village where Ovuru Ndiki signed his picture in my book on my earlier trip. It was sad to know he was gone now. The gallant, ageing World

War 2 Carrier was so frail when I saw him that to learn that he'd died 3 months later was ultimately expected. His soulful eyes still watch me.

An hour after our arrival, lunch was finished, and we were leaving Naduri, returning to the Track which taunted us all the way down the sheer gradient into the bowels of another divide. Specifically, each steep, treacherous step bled you dry of every physical resource.

Finally, it delivered us to Efogi Creek, where its inviting clear water crashed over a hundred boulders and rocks. We could hear its increasing turbulence, similar to Eora Creek, as we descended the mountain, crossing the log bridge before stopping for a break at the base of the dry, ancient waterfall.

This was my nemesis, the part of the entire trek that unnerved me, with the sensation of its exhaustion continuing to haunt my resilience. It was as steep as I remembered, and I identified the places where Ladiva helped me, especially where I ground to a halt. Every step came back to me. Surprisingly easier, this climb was vastly assisted by devouring lunch at Naduri for some desperately needed fuel and the well-proven lollies before tackling the gauntlet.

We were met by Launanumu's villagers selling their string bags (bilums) to passing trekkers, but we kept going through the village, stopping briefly to read that unique memorial, the Seventh Day Adventist (SDA) monument, which I didn't get the chance to see last time.

Rain battered our weary party as we carefully negotiated the slippery Track down to Efogi. Now, so near to home and his newborn, James took Kathy by the hand, leading her at a pace down the divots of the worn path, an astonishing feat. Poor Kathy was almost like a rag doll following him on pure reflex down the hill. She told me later that James must have been thinking that her slow pace *cannot go on!* She is such good value, and we get on so well; what a laugh. You meet the most amazing people in the most phenomenal places...a freak gravitating of sorts.

I took some wet clothes over to the Hot House (or Drying Hut) I remembered from last time to have them dried out for 20 Kina in PNG currency; a luxury, but a handy one. The souls of my feet hurt from the thick, wet hiking socks, it seems, so it will be great to finally dry them. Why are they wet...'cause this is the Kokoda Track, and they are!

Spaghetti Bolognese was gratefully enjoyed by all tonight, and we find ourselves camped in the same high-set long hut as last time, overlooking the museum. The Gekkos team is close by in a similar hut, but we'll meet up with them briefly tomorrow morning before they leave for Manari.

EFOGI - MANARI (29 April 2015)

This morning started with cereal, lollies and coffee for breakfast before having a look through the museum. They've possibly added to the collection since last time, although I'm not sure what exactly. They would obviously be adding to the collection regularly.

Leaving Efogi a short while after Gekkos, the landmarks of the Rangers Station, hospital, and Efogi airstrip were our last contact with Barnabas' home, the peaceful village where I hope to teach. And then it began...downhill, slippery and nasty, to the gentle creek crossing before climbing to the perfect vantage point overlooking Efogi. Cliff and I had Chris take our photo as we sat together on a fallen log. Then, in another few minutes, we were gone, wending our way along that section of the Track's rocky hillside I love so much before finally reaching Brigade Hill. This time there were no flags.

We remembered our brave fallen and paid tribute to them at the monument, a short break of reflection which also provided the perfect opportunity to buy some more bananas from the market hut across the clearing; those same sweet, tasty bananas, and always, *always* the best ones you will ever find. Then it was down, down, down over slippery, clay-like, sticky mud and tree roots – guaranteed that none of it has changed in countless millennia.

I see myself and everyone I was with two years ago at the places where we stopped for water breaks, Ladiva pointing to the safe spots to tread and John up ahead, Len and all the guys...two identical trips, two vastly different atmospheres.

This is still a great trip, though, and I'm managing much better this time. Lollies at breakfast seem to be more successful than protein bars, as they don't digest fast enough to meet the challenge of these rugged ranges. Cliff's also holding up quite well, and, oh, dry socks – I can't *believe* the difference!

We passed a large party of trekkers at a very muddy stretch and soon caught up with Naomi from the Gekkos group. She's done her knee, suffering terribly with the pain as a result, so her porter, Andy, was partly carrying her. To help keep herself focused, Naomi was asking him some words in his language and learnt that *good morning* in Motu is *daba namona.*

Undaunted, she was determined that we keep going and not let her hold us up, so leaving Naomi in Andy's skilled care, we passed her until she caught up with us down at the resting spot a little while later.

She was in tears by then, her imploring eyes breaking my heart in that moment. I gave her some lollies for comfort as much as energy, Anthony supplied her with Panadol, and after a while, she bravely continued on ahead. By the time we met up again at Vabiavu River, our next crossing, the Panadol had kicked in, and Naomi was managing better.

Once we arrived at Manari, some of us went to see one of the last Fuzzy Wuzzy Angels, Saii Faole's father, Faole Bokoi. I had given Barnabas my photos of Faole and his wife, Ovela

Hotoki, from my last trip to give to the veteran, not knowing I would actually see him, so Barna gave them to him later. Kathy took photos of me with him, but I didn't see Saii's mother this time. I hope she is well.

Cliff caught up on some much-needed sleep instead, but later, he, Kathy and I thoroughly enjoyed swimming in the nearby creek, a refreshing joy every time.

Some of our group are camped in tents as there isn't enough room for all of us, but Cliff, Kathy, Margaret, Tony, Rick, Tash, Naomi, and I are all in the hut together. It's a little cramped, but we're all good.

The kids had the best time throwing the frisbees Michael had given them while Tash strapped Naomi's knee. Tash is a physiotherapist, and they run a gym together, so Naomi's in good hands. After the vision of her today, it is nothing short of miraculous that she has even marginally improved after a couple of hours' rest.

Another storm, having rolled in briefly, can still be heard kicking around in the distance, drawing drifting clouds through the mountains and shrouding them with drizzling rain. Tranquillity continues to envelop us as we listen to the restless creek cascading into the depths of the rocky mountainside.

What a beautiful sight...*perfect* is this.

> *Saii Faole broke the sad news to me the following year in April 2016 that his father, Faole Bokoi, Chief of Manari Village, passed away on 10 March 2016.*

MANARI - NAURO (30 April 2015)

Cliff and I, complete with my bleary eyes, wished our youngest brother, Russ, a happy 57th birthday over our morning coffees. I only managed to get a couple of hours of sleep, having spent most of the night just looking at the view in between the flashes of lightning. It couldn't have been more irresistible.

We left Manari at the usual time of 6:30 am with a fairly wholesome climb straight up *The Wall* to Ladavi Saddle. Those who had Weetbix struggled a bit as it sat so heavily in their stomachs. I stuck to lollies basically, and while they're not especially nourishing, they do the job. What I'd give for a potato-top pie with mushy peas right now, though.

We all eventually regrouped on our break, overlooking the stunning Brown River Valley shrouded with clouds that hung lazily in its folds. At the right time and with warm updrafts feeding the conditions, these clouds rapidly develop into those rolling afternoon storms I love so much.

Then we faced the other side, slipping most of the way amongst even more tree roots to get to *the mud*. It was just as I remembered. It's a different terrain, more of a swamp, and it hasn't changed a bit, although I didn't mind the mud so much as the makeshift logs that acted as bridges. I was waiting to slip off with every step, as boots aren't flexible enough to grip the curve of logs, but somehow, I didn't fall; one of those miracles. Cliff's boot went down between the logs at this point, he told us later and felt the mud go over his gaiters and seep down into his boots.

That same incessant mud met us full-on for what seemed an endless time until we finally crossed the Brown River. A little higher than last time, our porters took us through the waist-high water, boots and all. It was a shame to get the inside of our boots completely wet, but there was no point in removing them. It's all murky here. In actual fact, no one stays here; it's steeped in legends and mystery and not a happy place.

After the mud, it was more uphill but manageable. For others, not quite so manageable, but we got here; Nauro Village, one of my favourite little villages, and still as pretty as a picture. I don't know...how many favourites can you have?

The water has been running intermittently as if regulated by a timer, and we had showers as they became available. Then came lunch; pasta, corned beef, tuna, baked beans and Pringle potato chips...and *necessary*.

A storm rolled in very quickly, causing us to gather our gear which we hoped might dry. Watching the clouds swirling in through the mountains as this afternoon's storm built up held a captivating beauty of its own. Everyone knows that from time to time, I become completely absorbed in my thoughts and this hushed presence; Nauro is one of those places that engulfs me in that headspace. It did it to me on the last trip, and I couldn't fight it this time, either. It is the mountains, the storms and the palpable quiet that fills me. The singing is noticeably missing this time, though, as it added to the magic of this beautiful place, giving it a heartbeat of its own.

The Gekko group will split off from us tomorrow and arrive at Owers Corner a day ahead of us, and we won't see them again. Naomi pulled up surprisingly well today, thankfully, and managed so much better than both she and I expected. Cliff and I had another photo taken together at a little village before Brown River, a charming little spot that I couldn't remember visiting previously. More rain has come in, so with the mountains shrouded in clouds, once again, we're all just resting up to the sound of heavy showers.

Mashed potato for tea...absolutely wonderful! I shamelessly went back for seconds. My freezing shower was also a gift, that perfect gem in the rough, and I'm presently drying my eternally mud-stained socks over the fire. How I love this place.

NAURO – IORIBAIWA (01 May 2015)

We coo-eed the Gekkos in farewell as we watched our mates heading up Maguli Ridge at 6:00 am; we won't see them again from here on. There is no singing in the mornings or at water stops, but my connection here fills me completely. Long after slipping and struggling in the mud and tree roots, I will continue to miss these ranges beyond words and am pulled two ways knowing this trek will soon end.

This time I was fully prepared for the steep climb through evermore sticky mud and seemingly endless tree roots lacing the interminable gradient. Newton was superb at every step and has been phenomenal the entire way. The poor man is exhausted without showing it, an exhausting task in itself.

We stopped at the zigzag trenches long enough for photos that promise to be clearer than last time, and Cliff disappeared with Chris to view more trenches nearby. I preferred to save my feet instead, a decision I might regret, but my photos capture the trenches in dappled sunlight illuminating the greenery and occasional orange foliage. I don't think I got it wrong.

Since arriving at Ioribaiwa's pretty camp around 1:30 pm after lunch at Ofi Creek, a brief storm rumbled in to roar at us, and another is threatening, with its clouds rolling in around us like mist and the thunder inching nearer.

These peaceful mountains surrounding us, the place where Roger Stedman and the 2/25 Battalion joined the fray, once rang with intense gunfire heaping death, and now we visualise these hard-fought battles and our Boys' muddy, bloody state. They were still outnumbered 5 to 1 before their fighting withdrawal to Imita Ridge, where they would wait, stretching the Japanese defences even thinner, void of all reinforcements, supplies and hope.

After washing our muddy gear and cleaning up in the picturesque shower overlooking the mountains across the valley (I am replicating this shower at home!), we settled back for a restful afternoon.

The guys brought us popcorn which thoroughly hit the spot, followed a little later by a dinner of pasta and braised steak and onions. We are all just sitting around watching the clouds and lightning now. There is just no end to this magic.

IORIBAIWA – UAULE (02 May 2015)

We were about to leave at 06:30 am, and the minister came over to bless us. I don't know how many roosters crowed to the full moon the entire night, but I'm surprised there weren't a few less by morning. I laugh, but I actually didn't mind. They aren't as raucous as screeching fruit bats.

Thomas, our lead guy, led us out of Ioribaiwa past the memorial commemorating the battle here. This was where the Japanese lay their last offensive upon our troops in 1942. The long-range guns that our Boys had physically dragged up to the summit of Imita Ridge were trained on Ioribaiwa, effectively raining long-range hell down on the enemy. The battle was hard-fought, and our troops continued with their defensive withdrawal strategy, digging in at Imita Ridge before returning to hammer the Japanese all the way back into the sea.

Drawn like a magnet to the monument, we commemorated their heroism, feeling very fortunate for the vast knowledge Chris shared with us until Thomas prompted our descent to the creek crossings, where boots came off to be replaced by joggers. Their flexibility made managing the temporarily docile Track practically effortless, and walking through the tropical, fern-shrouded water courses reignited those familiar senses for this primal stretch of scenery.

On our way down, Thomas and Newton pointed out a Bird of Paradise, although it was difficult to detect, being partly obscured by branches and leaves. At least I saw it.

Eventually, we came to the last creek crossing, and our boots went back on, ready for the climb up to Imita Ridge. Lollies here; *many* lollies! I still feel the sensation of my last brutal climb up the Ridge, and it certainly hasn't changed. It was intense, but I felt really good and managed well.

I don't feel I've struggled so much this time and am particularly encouraged that I would go from Owers Corner if I were to do the Track again. It's the fistful of lollies and chocolates at the base of an ascent, in addition to the glucodin and hydrolytes, that have made the difference - I think I'm as fit now as I was the first time, although not fitter.

The mud is utterly, *utterly* monotonous now, and it's a long stretch over some of those logs and tree roots...well, for us shorties, anyway. Cliff looked shagged when we reached the top of Imita Ridge, and he's had some fair busters along the way. There was some signal by then, so the message to Saii was for a cold carton of SP Lager to greet us on our arrival at Owers Corner, so there's something to look forward to!

Margaret seems the greatest surprise, though, our wiry 75-year-old, who has been truly remarkable. Michael is keen to go home; I would go so far as saying he's already there by the pained look on the poor man's face.

Rick filed along ahead of us all, coming down the other side with his porter, so he arrived in camp way ahead of us. He reckons he'd do the Track again but without poles and from Owers Corner. Anthony isn't so keen and will be grateful for some roast pork and crackling with all the trimmings...*and an early plane out of town!*

Kathy is fantastic and, being an anaesthetist, is normally well-scrubbed up so reckons she's never felt so filthy. It's my guess she'll be prepped and ready for theatre one day, and think randomly about being covered in the Track's mud and grime, only to race out and scrub up again. We have had such a laugh together.

Cliff's currently asleep...no...he just moved. He's absolutely busted. Rick picked up some meagre signal and broke the news that a 7.8 magnitude earthquake struck Nepal on Anzac

Day with growing numbers of fatalities. He is booked to climb Everest Base Camp in August, but all Base Camp treks are presently cancelled. Kathy and Margaret have both trekked Nepal's Annapurna Trail, another must-do experience I hope to adore.

We swam in Uaule Creek, sorted out our muddy gear, and enjoyed this afternoon's rain storm where I sat simply immersed in the downpour for almost an hour, absorbing the serenity like it was therapy. Noodles and all the usual accompaniments warmed us through at lunch, although I don't think I will have noodles again for a while!

Uaule is slightly different to last time (relocated maybe), but we're ringed by 360 degrees of mountains, and it leaves me speechless. Another storm kicks around out there, and right now, clouds are creeping in through the mountains again.

After tea, we sat around talking and watching the fireflies flickering everywhere...literally *hundreds* of them. I couldn't believe what I was seeing – another in the long list of unforgettable moments. Tragically, though, fireflies perform this spectacle as they are about to die, leaving a breathtaking moment in time that lasts forever, the perfect enigma in a place of lost souls.

UAULE – OWERS CORNER (03 May 2015)

Getting away at 6:30 am, we encountered a muddy and slippery track after last night's torrential rain, but comparatively good plodding.

Goldie River was as enchanting as ever, and I laughed quietly at the memory of falling in, the sensation so strong I briefly transported to the moment. Newton was there, ever-ready to help, so I was unlikely to repeat the mishap, as inviting as the entertaining thought might be. This was also where we had a short break before heading up to Owers Corner, our final climb.

There were a couple of stops along the way as our porters dutifully went ahead to prepare for our exit through those magnificent Owers Corner arches. And then it came, that almost surreal wonder when I looked up and saw their crests. We were there.

When we topped the hill beneath them, we found our porters presented in a Guard of Honour blessing our safe arrival with their beautiful singing. Saii was there too, and true to his word, had put on SPs for the drive down to Port Moresby...we were half drunk by 9:45 am!

Too early to check into the motel, we spent some time meandering throughout Bomana War Cemetery for a better look, although Cliff couldn't find the coordinates Victor had given him. Chris showed us Bruce Kingsbury and Butch Bisset's graves which was quite moving as I'd read about them so often in Patrick's book, and John had taken my photo at Kingsbury's Rock commemorating Kingsbury's valiant stand at Isurava.

When it was time, we headed back to the Holiday Inn Express for welcome hot showers followed by a fabulous lunch at the restaurant, just Rick, Tony, Cliff and me; burgers and chips for them, and a Mexican tostada and baked potato with sour cream for me. There was nothing quite like it.

All the guys came back for beer and pizzas around 5:00 pm, and John came with them. We had a great catch-up, and I gave him my State of Origin shirt. Out of nowhere, he presented me with a beautiful bilum, as well as one from Ladiva who couldn't be there, both generously made by their families at home.

Newton made me a stunning Kokoda 2015 Anzac Day Tour carving, charred over the fire with the words carved meticulously into the wood. I have to believe I won't lose it at customs. I gave Newton 50 Kina (PNG K50), some medical supplies and whatever lollies I had left, and that was all I had for this gentle man who saw me safely through mud, rocks, logs, and every other living hell the Track delivered at our trudging feet.

I also managed to get everyone to sign my *Kokoda Spirit* book on the back cover and my shirt as well. It was a great night, and we all exchanged email addresses and contact details.

After the guys had gone home on the bus to their villages, we simply sat back sharing stories for a couple of hours, and wouldn't you know it, two of our mates from the Gekkos turned up. All went well with their group, also, after putting in some long days to arrive at Owers Corner 24 arduous hours earlier.

I am coming back, and I won't settle until I can spend more time here teaching these kids, starting with Efogi.

Records show Corporal Cecil Mervyn Pikett, QX50250, was transferred with serious burns from Bougainville to Port Moresby, where he died on 29 March 1945. However, his Mother/Widows Badge was issued in 1944 on his death.

* * *

Barnabas Omi and Tommy Mado crossing Eora Ck Bridge 2015.

Myola 2015

Cliff (left) with Chris, his porter and historian, crossing the Vabiavu River 2015.

From left. Mike, Kathy, Rick, Ruth, Margaret, Cliff and Tony at Brigade Hill 2015.

Faole Bokoi revisited at Manari 2015.

Crossing the Brown River swamp 2015.
Photograph courtesy of Cliff James.

The Efogi cutting on the way to Brigade Hill 2015.

The treacherous climb to Imita Ridge 2015.
Photograph courtesy of Cliff James.

Newton between Kokoda and Hoi 2015.

Chapter 3

Efogi 2017

> EFOGI VILLAGE – 21 April to 4 May 2017

I have a motto discreetly tattooed, and I like it; *Never say never*. And this is a perfect example of why.

Within six months of starting my TESOL Course with Inspire Education, I attained my internationally accredited certification to teach non-English speaking students. Without it, I couldn't have made this trip. In fact, my certificate was signed-off three days earlier, so I was not wasting time!

Emails, itineraries and transactions with Saii Faole have brought this momentous trip together, and I couldn't have managed it without him.

This is my dream. Since I first walked the brutal Track, I have yearned for this moment, now I live it.

So, yes, n*ever say never*.

PORT MORESBY – 21 APRIL 2017 (FRIDAY)

Finally, here at the Holiday Inn Express, Port Moresby, I'm all checked in and sorted out. The shuttle was waiting at the Jackson International Airport exit, and the only other passenger sharing the ride was fellow trekker and world traveller, Sandy Munro. Tomorrow, she flies to Alotau, the *go-to* place in Milne Bay, for a few days' vacation, then comes back for the Dawn Service ahead of the Anzac Day Trek from Kokoda end with the South Sea Horizons boys.

Hailing from South Australia, Everest Base Camp has been Sandy's favourite trek a number of times, but her last much-anticipated trip to Mt Everest was unimaginably shattered; Nepal, Anzac Day, 2015.

Sandy survived the catastrophic Nepal earthquake when it levelled the village near her camp, killing approximately 9,000 people in the region. Base Camp was instantly off-limits. All communication was gone.

Instead, Sandy entered a broken world, rescuing survivors and assisting in recoveries for seemingly endless days; my God, the exhaustion, the courage! This humble and compassionate human being is truly something else. Rick's announcement of the earthquake when Cliff and I were at Uaule came back to me all at once; little could I have known.

Tomorrow, Alotau's picturesque coastline on the Eastern tip of PNG will be Sandy's home away from home in a remote village that requires a canoe to get there, her short break before heading up the Track.

Prior to my briefing with Saii on tomorrow's arrangements, I re-organised some of my gear for easier access, discovering shortly after that there has been a change of plans.

I fly to Efogi on Sunday as the helicopter pilot is SDA and doesn't work on Saturdays, so I've had to book another night here at the Holiday Inn Express.

Dinner was Spinach Lasagne over the road at the Holiday Inn, big brother to the Express, and thoroughly enjoyable. After my meeting with Saii, Sandy and I met up again for a couple of drinks and a long chat, talking for hours. I'll be at Efogi when she comes through, so we're looking forward to catching up again then. If I'm awake in time in the morning, I'll have coffee with her before she leaves. This whole trip is just going to be great!

22 APRIL 2017 (SATURDAY)

Having slept uncharacteristically soundly through my first night back, I didn't get to see Sandy before she left, but right now, I'm sure she's stoked on her way to the airport for Alotau. In my own enthusiasm, I headed down to breakfast, a flavour-filled buffet with everything, including the greatest coffee. Nothing beats a great coffee.

Saii caught up with me around mid-morning, having arranged transport for tomorrow's 6:00 am start to take me to the airport ahead of an hour-long helicopter ride; Manari first, then Manari 2 (near Brigade Hill), arriving at Efogi last. This will be my first time up in a helicopter, and I can't wait.

Spending the rest of the day reviewing lessons for my 2-week syllabus, this afternoon's efforts kept me relatively busy. I discovered I will be teaching Grades 6 and 8 students, but maybe I can have some younger grades in there, too – I have material for them all, covering all classes. And it will be so.

Anzac Day's Dawn Service will be held at the haunting Brigade Hill Memorial, so I will join the families and trekkers hiking in the dark to attend. Who knows how I'm going to pull up after it, or even manage at all, considering I haven't trained except for a few 4km runs in the past few weeks, which doesn't constitute training. I'll just have to put in a couple of climbs up the hill behind the Drying Hut or down to the river and back. That will at least help.

As the Port Moresby heat shimmered across the numerous rooftops overlooked by the fourth floor, the view out to the Owen Stanleys was as exciting as ever, and from the hotel's back patio, I watched one of PNG's compelling storms flashing away as the warm dusk gave way to the cooler evening air.

I have returned.

23 APRIL 2017 (SUNDAY)

It didn't take me long to gather myself and my few morning items and settle in downstairs by 5:25 am. Saii collected Alice Ijuri along the way arriving just a little while later. Alice is a health worker returning to Efogi Hospital, and we hit it off immediately. Her gentle nature has a lively edge, and she is such a laugh. Like Sandy, we get on extraordinarily well.

There was a blue at the airport, too. One of the locals reckoned he'd paid his freight and wanted to collect it, but his docket showed the consignment remained outstanding, so he was going right off. A tall Australian guy was handling it in Pidgin, but eventually, he'd had enough, saying *Here, take all your gear and bugger off!* So typically Australian.

Alice generously offered me the front seat, an unexpected surprise, to join Wade, our Gold Coast pilot, who is now a PNG local of three years. It was wild, though. The helicopter topped the ridge before the jungle-covered slope dropped steeply into the valley below, the very vision of it giving me that freaky elevator sensation you get from a sudden plunge, although it was purely optical. Wade landed in the middle of the village's vast, empty sports field, the perfect landing pad, an event that created great interest and soon had us surrounded by Efogi's excited villagers. *Never say never.*

Saii had radioed ahead as Barnabas Omi was waiting for me before heading up the Track to meet his party of trekkers at Kokoda – Sandy's group. He was thrilled I was finally here, and it was wonderful to see him, even if only briefly. A number of the guys from the crowd that had gathered collected all my gear, including the two weeks of supplies Saii had arranged.

Barnabas had kindly organised my billet with the Lovai's, the headmaster's family, and before he hurried off, I thanked the good-hearted man for this rare opportunity. Although the headmaster is away, his wife, Narni, and three boys, Guru (10), Vella (8) and Caleb (2), have all made me feel so welcome. In the most thoughtful gesture, Narni insisted that I take their own room, dismissing my protests. Not wanting to intrude, I was content to bunk down anywhere, but this generous woman wasn't having any of it.

The high-set house hosts a front verandah to hang the washing and a metre-wide walkway alongside cut out of the embankment. Earthen steps lead up to the open grass between two more huts; the head teacher's house is on the left, and the other, a disused teacher's quarters that remains temporarily neglected. My head bursts with ideas just looking at it!

Separate from the house, the well-organised kitchen is arranged around the central firepit/oven, with the family's stores of vegetables and other produce filling the corner table. The view from the push-out window over the colourful shrubs makes the sink perfectly placed with a cupboard stocked with PNG tea and other dry staples conveniently alongside.

In the glow of the warm family atmosphere, Guru cooked some rice, pasta and choko leaves while I opened a couple of tins of tuna and corned beef for a hot lunch. He's an experienced cook for a 10-year-old, and the rice was perfectly steamed...something I can't always get right.

Unpacking my remaining supplies during the afternoon quiet, I discovered Saii provided me with that distinctive Track food, its familiar sight making me smile and feel right at home. And if that isn't enough, there is an even greater wonder.

From my window, I contentedly look out to the Track to watch intermittent streams of porters and villagers heading up from the river crossing to that pretty cutting I love so much along the hillside. This trip is a sheer privilege.

Guru and Vella escorted me down the Track to the Nurse's Station on the outskirts of the village, where they left me with Alice to catch up again for a few hours as arranged, another enjoyable chance to talk.

Showing me around the hospital, Alice explained there'd been a birth in one of the wards a few days earlier. She has only recently taken over her accommodation and has been transforming her garden at the back of the house. What was once in need of attention is swiftly becoming a lush source of rich, green produce nourished by the abundant rains.

A storm is coming in over the mountain nearby, and we, over 400 Efogi villagers and one extra Australian, are entirely enveloped in clouds…it is everything I knew it would be.

24 APRIL 2017 (MONDAY)

A great day today, although heralded by an uncertain start. The bell was rung for worship, bringing with it a steady line of villagers on their way to the long timber church.

I learned later that the kids have been on their school holidays, with all the teachers still in Moresby for Anzac Day and not returning until Wednesday.

The surprise news continued when Narni told me the kids arrived for school because I am here, but there is no key to the classrooms until the Head Teacher returns. For now, all the classrooms are locked, so I can't do anything classroom-orientated, anyway.

On explaining this to Pastor Samuel, we arranged that I would wait for the teachers to return before accessing the classrooms, improvising instead by holding classes out in the old kitchen, that pretty thatched bamboo hut next to the house. It is perfect and convenient with its bench seats and tables. In fact, it could not be better.

Pastor Samuel is actually the same pastor who blessed us as Cliff and our party left Ioribaiwa two years ago. I remember the pastor's familiar face.

We're all good for tomorrow's Dawn Service at Brigade Hill. We leave at 3:30 am, so just to get the blood running in preparation, Guru, Vella, Wilma and Mary-Claire, the pastor's daughters, climbed with me to Launanumu. We also met Janette at her stall at the Efogi signpost, and Vella took a lovely photo of Janette and me before we returned home for lunch.

I introduced the boys to my board games, specially designed by me for vocabulary, grammar, and descriptive writing, as well as a Trivial Pursuit card game which Narni enjoyed with us. The boys were thoroughly absorbed, requesting more games and soaking up the knowledge. More importantly, they were retaining this wholesome information through this novel technique untried in their school.

Guru and I cooked pasta and some chicken that one of the neighbours gave us, later sharing stories that revealed the boys' hopes for the future. We also talked for hours about World War 2 and general history, sharing an all-round interactive day.

Another storm came in mid-afternoon, as it does, compelling a lone firefly to emerge flickering outside the old kitchen, immediately transporting me to that spell-binding moment in Uaule where we watched them in their hundreds.

Hours later, the same storm continues to hang in the valleys out there in the dark, its frequent flashes blazing momentarily around the room like flashlights.

ANZAC DAY - 25 APRIL 2017 (TUESDAY)

Our morning started at 2:30 am, meeting with the others from the village at Pastor Samuel's house for the 3:30 am hike up to Brigade Hill, guided by the light from our headlamps. There was a bit of confusion for a while, but we finally got away. I was waiting for Alice, her son, and two sisters, Veronica (Ronnie) and Josephine, as I'd promised to walk with them, but I was obligated to head off with the others seeing she hadn't arrived. It was believed she'd gone ahead instead.

It hadn't rained on this side of the mountain through the night, so although it was still slippery, it wasn't treacherous. After the *down*, there was the *up, up, up,* flattening intermittently as I recalled my earlier trips, the thoughts filling my mind almost reverently. The *up* from there was decidedly more manageable, which was fortunate considering I hadn't trained. Interestingly, the terrain felt different at night under the glow of headlamps, like it was a mysterious underworld, not the green jungle full of life.

I accompanied the pastor, his wife and his son, Malaki, arriving at the monument on time, the Papuan and Australian flags both motionless on either side in the calm darkness. Vella had followed a little way behind with the family, or so I thought. It turned out to be Alice and her family, after all, who had fallen in behind us as we passed the hospital.

Yesterday's storm had flashed all night and was still illuminating the room even as we were rising, so it was unsurprising that the same storm flashed out in the distance. Below us, the trailing clouds lay suspended in the valleys as the Dawn Service began to the sounds of faraway thunder. It was beautiful in every sense, and there was not a dry eye throughout the ceremony. The Papuan singing was breathtaking as always, and a smaller service was held by the Salvation Army, convenient for anyone arriving too late for the first.

Returning in daylight was much easier than in darkness, and yet the unforgettable experience will stay with me along with a hundred others.

Arriving back at Efogi meant an early lunch of biscuits, avocado and cheese for me, with the others enjoying the tinned fish and peas I gave them to accompany their rice. It has been a long time since mashed potato and corned beef have been on my menu, so this will be my dinner tonight - my ultimate Track special.

Two of my favourite worlds collide right here; I am in the middle of the rugged and bloodied Kokoda Track *and* living my dream teaching its isolated children. Some of my students will be quite young, apparently, so they should love the activities I've brought for them, including the alphabet train, a catchy little activity.

An interschool volleyball, soccer, and touch football carnival was held this afternoon in the open area where my chopper landed, with teams travelling from Kovolo, a few kilometres up the Track, to attend. We may bleat endlessly about the Track's harshness, but these visitors returned to Kovolo when the last game finished, a typical walk for everyone here, with most arriving home in the dark. That said, there was much cheering and laughter throughout the games making for a relaxed and light-hearted afternoon.

After the games, I took a little time to do my washing in the river past the house, using soap and scrubbing my clothes against one of the boulders. It's a social activity generally, with everyone sharing time to swim and wash. Two of the young girls wanted to help, so we happily started talking and washing the clothes together.

Clouds rolled in over the ranges while I was at the river, and another storm rumbles out in the distance as I write. In the true essence of this remote culture, the kids carry a broad leaf, similar to a Caladium or Elephant's Ear, as an umbrella when it's raining, perfect for keeping these small children dry. It is a beautiful thing to see.

Sleep now - 6:10 p.m.

26 APRIL 2017 (WEDNESDAY)

I decided to attend the early morning service at 6:30 am to engage better with the Efogi Community and for them to become more comfortable with me. Pastor Samuel conducted the sermon in Efogi's mother tongue, as well as Pidgin and a little English, but it came as no surprise to discover a hymn isn't a hymn until you've heard it sung in that magical style that belongs to these gentle people. Equally as touching, a blessing was held for the teachers, including me, making me feel so very welcome and a trusted guest in their community.

Narni and I talked together like we'd known each other for years, simply enjoying our walk back to the house where the boys had made a hardy fire for our coffees. We shared words in Motu, stories of how their Port Moresby family came to be here for the past few months and would be returning home to the city in two years. Naturally, teachers and headmasters are posted to all corners of the Provinces, as are nurses and various other professions.

It was during this relaxed conversation that James Enage, CEO of the Kokoda Track Authority (KTA), braved a rushed visit to welcome me on his way to the airfield from Launanumu as distant thuds preceded the imminent arrival of the chopper taking him to Port Moresby. News had reached him that the school remained closed, requiring improvised lessons to be held in the hut instead, a situation which prompted genuine apologies from this great man.

Assuring him the lessons were not impeded but the great success I had hoped, he gave me his business card in farewell before breathlessly hurrying off to meet the chopper landing at the outskirts of the village.

After making a breakfast of Weetbix and apricot jam for the family and cornflakes and coffee for me, I explained more of the board games to the boys; the Australian states and their capital cities as well as our flora and fauna, and my customised *True or False* game with its 50 vocabulary, grammar and numeracy questions. Happily playing for hours, the kids maintained a keen interest, their curiosity stimulated by the lessons' creativity.

Pastor Samuel visited and enjoyed watching the boys playing the board game, and we made some wonderful inroads toward future trips. He listened to my ideas and was very encouraging. I can be set up in all the villages along the Track and in other villages also. I explained I will bring books for their libraries on future trips or alternatively, I'd find a way to send them. Pastor understands my situation financially and personally, knowing I may not be back for a while after this, but the plans are falling into place, and he wants me to see the Mission Director of the Central Papua Conference (CPC) before I leave Moresby.

I intended to go down to the river below Launanumu today, but time got away from me. It's raining now with another storm kicking around, and the boys are cooking some rice and sweet potato (kau kau), perfect for the curried chicken sauce I will open to go with it.

It is almost 4:00 pm, and it is beautiful.

27 APRIL 2017 - THURSDAY

Guru, Vella, Ronnie, Josephine and I met here at the house to follow the divets up the hillside to Launanumu before carefully descending to Efogi Creek, my first venture to the river from this side of the Track. This walk was clearly different, although the same rocks and ferns lay etched throughout the narrow track, with the one creek crossing our path numerous times. Cool skin soon gave way to sweat as the cardio cut in, but the entire walk was so much more beautiful than I remembered. The climb's intensity overpowered that memory.

The river rushing over the rocks a few hundred metres below beckoned our arrival, and the naturally sure-footed kids immediately made their way to their favourite boulders alongside the low bamboo bridge. Photos, photos, photos - there just had to be photos - then some lunch I'd packed for us before we reluctantly considered climbing home.

This was the very climb that walked me to a standstill back in 2013, the dry waterfall's rock face, although my last trip was infinitely easier. So armed with lollies, once again, I was fine, not even sore muscles.

Back, again, at Efogi, the older girls headed home to the hospital, politely declining the invitation to stay, and I brought out the cards for Vella, Guru, and Wilma to play *Snap* with me, although a little bit of cheating went on there, I'm sure. We also cooled off in the creek behind the house to freshen up before returning for more.

Once the game started, kids from all around wanted to join in, so I left them to it, coming back upstairs to help Narni with the clothes and Caleb. More rain was coming.

A surprise visit from John livened up the late afternoon, revealing that Barnabas bumped into him along the Track at Alola and told him I was here. This was completely unexpected, giving us a chance to share all our news. His party commemorated Anzac Day at Isurava, a stunning memorial at any time, but in the eerie quiet of dawn, I could only imagine its haunting serenity. John doesn't work for South Sea Horizons any more, trekking instead for another company that includes Popondetta in its itinerary, where he flew recently for a Northern

Beaches Trek. Ladiva and Chris have also made recent career changes, now working for the Electrical Board.

The visit was interrupted an hour or so later by a storm fairly close by, so, still in disbelief, we exchanged hugs of best wishes and safe travels for his journey to Owers Corner. His pre-dawn departure will be represented by his bobbing head-lamp across the valley as he makes his way up the Track in the dark. It was so good of him to call in, and my first endeavour is to thank Barnabas for this marvellous surprise when he arrives with Sandy's party.

After the day's excitement, I had an early evening with the family as thunder rolled endlessly through the hills behind the house, all quiet and locked.

28 APRIL 2017 (FRIDAY)

It's been another treasured day and a joy to be here with this beautiful family. Yet another reason to love these generous people comes from the kindness of an elderly lady who brought me some bananas, a treat I shared before a soccer game with Wilma, Guru and Vella at the school's playing field. We have so much fun together. Guru was keen to learn my favourite move, a creative side step I practised many times during my limited soccer career, although I am sure his edge will bring the trick deserving mileage.

The teachers won't be back from Moresby for a few days, so I'll continue our English games in the hut. I hear different reports of their return, one of the more promising being that they should arrive Monday, all going well. There may even be one returning tomorrow - don't know.

Vella and I went for a walk down to the village in the late afternoon to see if Sandy's party had arrived, conceding it would probably be tomorrow instead. Otherwise, they would be flaked out on the floor of their hut or any convenient bench as wet gear dripped at random from the verandah. It wasn't until after dark that a familiar voice outside called Narni, and to my greatest surprise, it was Barnabas (whom I thanked) and Sandy with another girl from their group, Kelly Gatt. It was a thrill to finally see them, and as I always have my headlamp ready around my neck after sundown, we four immediately headed down to that familiar hut overlooking the museum to catch up. The bugs were out in their droves, coming in ahead of another storm; I was sure I was going to swallow one!

Their trek is going to plan with no disasters, thankfully, and Sandy's porter is my very own Newton from last time! This is sheer coincidence, and as expected, the caring man is as wonderful with her as he was with me.

Kelly, a much-adored High School teacher, suggested an aid group that might be able to put me onto a team that provides assistance with aid along the Track, so I've given her my email address, and she'll send through details. Another girl, Michelle Rayner from the Navy, joined us as we sat together talking for over an hour, blanketed by dense clouds.

When Kelly asked my thoughts on the most difficult climbs, two immediately sprang to mind. I assured them they were over the first one, with the other a few days away...lacey, brutal Imita Ridge. I believe my words described the unforgiving wall as *stone-cold and motherless.* They'd come this far and were smashing it, though, so my best advice was to get that energy fix in at the bottom of the climb, and they would sail the rest. Or at least they couldn't go wrong.

Sandy and Kelly leave Moresby before my return, so we have each other's details to keep in touch. I would love to climb Everest Base Camp with Sandy one day or perhaps hike Nepal's nearby Anapurna Trail. *Never say never.*

Promising to see them off at dawn, I headed home, knowing Sandy was travelling well. For this extraordinary woman, The

Kokoda Track now takes its own defiant stance alongside the anniversary of Nepal's fatal earthquake.

Kelly later embraced a game-changing career, running her own business as a Contract Concreter. Thought to be the first licensed female concreter in Australia, her leadership and inspiration are beacons to follow.

29 APRIL 2017 (SATURDAY)

As arranged, I was up early to meet the group before they left, taking Newton's photos from my last trip with me. Barnabas disappeared briefly, bringing Newton and Ian Kero back with him, and like John, it was exciting to see them both. We only had time for a quick catch-up as the group was almost ready to leave following their 2-minute call. Just hearing the words *Two minutes!* took my right back. I turned to Barnabas with a knowing smile, and he simply laughed.

And so, after a couple of photos, it was time. They were loaded up and on their way, weary and bleary-eyed, the pretty cutting alongside the hill being their next stopping point before the slog up Mission Ridge to Brigade Hill.

Following the weary trekkers' poignant departure, Efogi Village and its gentle community shared their Saturday of worship with me. I maintain a spiritual outlook on life, although I personally don't need to pray in a church, or at all for that matter, but unexplainable experiences that defy physics, logic and all odds, have convinced me there is a power beyond our limited understanding, a power we don't have to understand, only that it is there. Whatever *it* is.

However we uphold our beliefs is entirely personal, and the gentle people of Papua New Guinea uphold theirs in a truly respectful and peaceful love for each other and those from afar who bond with them. It was for this reason I joined their endearing community sharing three hours with them in church. Pastor Samuel is trying hard to *shanghai* me into the flock, but he also understands my beliefs. I'm sure he's not giving up on converting me, but good on him for trying.

A late lunch for me consisted of mashed potato, green peas and pork luncheon meat filled the spot my metabolism left craving. Later in the afternoon, I headed down to the creek to wash my hair and am just enjoying some quiet time during everyone's return to church.

30 APRIL 2017 (SUNDAY)

It's funny how I've spent three of Russ' last five birthdays in PNG, but then if I'm commemorating Anzac Day up here, then the 30th of April will swiftly follow.

Subsequently, here I am again, wishing him a happy birthday, only this time from Efogi.

This morning was the perfect lie-in while Narni and Caleb went to worship, rising an hour later to make Weet Bix with either peanut butter or plum jam for everyone. This old classic has now become *their* unexpected favourite.

By mid-morning, the boys were cleaning up the kitchen like they were on a mission, a massive job completed beautifully like clockwork. My own morning was spent in the old kitchen hut, going through items for lessons and adding ideas, etc. I also re-read my notes from the two previous trips, sentiments I later shared with Vella.

There has been a tragedy in Port Moresby; the death of a policeman from Naduri. Narni and I watched from the verandah as the helicopter made several trips over the mountains to bring his body home for burial. The numerous flights throughout the day brought family members, supplies and belongings, one specifically being the policeman's bell.

Surprising me with lunch while I was immersed in my work out in the hut, Narni brought over some hot corn freshly cooked over the fire and deliciously flavourful. If I'm honest, I can't ever remember eating corn so juicy and moreish, but then that's PNG's lush produce for you.

A growing number of kids came over when Claira arrived to play board games. They hadn't seen these English activities before, so others very quickly gathered around. The neighbour's 4-year-old boy, Milon, absorbed every move the players made, so it was unsurprising that he stayed behind when the others left. Fascinated by the pictures and rolling the dice, Milon counted every move along the board with the corresponding number on the dice, completely immersed. He knows his numbers, and we played until it was too dark to see. He waved happily to me when he left, and I watched him in the fading light as he ducked around the corner to his front steps about 15m away.

I only wish I'd been able to do this a long time ago, but better now than never.

01 MAY 2017 (MONDAY)

No teachers again, with their arrival unlikely now until Wednesday. In light of this, I have taken up Alice's kind offer of a supply of her butcher's paper to use in tomorrow morning's lessons in the hut, the news met with great excitement by a crowd of eager students. Seeing their enthusiasm for learning brought its own joy as they looked forward to it as much as I did.

Spending the morning with Ronnie, Josephine and Claira was vast amounts of fun. We turned one of the spare rooms down at the Medical Centre into a classroom, and Pastor Samuel paid us a visit watching the progress of the lesson with interest. Word games are so creative, and the girls loved this fresh perspective, as did Pastor Samuel. We covered homonyms, and conveniently, a perfect example was *pastor* and *pasta*, which clearly delighted the unsuspecting Pastor Samuel.

Alice informed me that the girls want me to be their 'foster' mother, which is so very sweet - I feel truly honoured. Shortly after the discussion, Josie and Ronnie came out of the house almost a little shyly until moments later, they were cheerfully wrapped in warm hugs. Family isn't always exclusively family.

Vella and I headed down to check in at the Ranger's Office about the ETA of the helicopter on the 4th - it should be around 6:30 am, but the ranger will confirm this. I just don't want to be forgotten and left behind with a plane to catch. Well, I do, really, but can't be.

Choko leaves, rice and kau kau for dinner this evening, a meal always thoroughly enjoyable, but tonight even more so. These river greens have *no* comparison. I still can't exactly place their flavour; somewhere between pakchoi and cabbage with a nuttiness I could devour at any meal.

02 MAY 2017 (TUESDAY)

And so it happened...my first complete Efogi class - 20 students!!

With the cooperation of Paster Samuel and the parents, my kitchen hut class was transformed when behold, a key to the school miraculously appeared, and with it, the opportunity to hold lessons in the long-awaited classroom.

Hugely successful, all my students engaged happily together; among them, the gentle academic Claira, who showed me her exquisite writing yesterday, Malakai, Jeff, young Freddie, Guru,

Vella, Wilma and Mari-Claire, although there were many others. Missing letters of the alphabet was my introductory lesson, followed by vowel flowers for word-forming from a group of consonants with one vowel, the alphabet game in four teams of five and making as many words from *retribution* as they could, anagrams to a point.

Divided into halves, the class worked on each side of the blackboard, resulting in a 40-word tie which was broken in the ensuing tie-breaker by Guru's triumphant detection. Pastor Samuel called in to observe the progress and was surprised at the volume of words the kids had derived from that one unassuming word. Everyone had the best time with more ahead as they look forward to tomorrow morning's recap on missing letters before getting creative with different animal features. They are in for a surprise classroom safari!

Finishing at noon after taking a few photos that the kids just had to see, I promised to send them copies for their school noticeboard. As they were technically still on holidays, we relaxed for the rest of the day after re-locking the classroom ready for tomorrow.

Pastor Samuel came up to see me, and we walked down to sit with his family, where he gave me some names and details for contacts that would assist my future trips. He was still in awe at the volume of words the kids were able to derive from one word and was enjoying the activity himself out of sheer curiosity. I think I enjoyed the delight on his face every bit as much as those in the kids' absorbed expressions. The Senior Teacher, Milon's father, returned today, so I should meet him later or possibly tomorrow.

Clouds are building over the mountains, so being 3:50 pm, it should rain soon. Vella and Narni spoke to me about teaching him to tell the time, and I gladly agreed to help.

While Narni and Guru took Caleb for a walk, we went through clockface configurations, and within 3/4 of an hour, Vella was telling the time confidently...and *proudly*. Narni couldn't believe the difference, and in truth, nor could he, as the task had seemed so hopelessly daunting. There is a lot to be said for a little uninterrupted time to learn without pressure.

03 MAY 2017 (WEDNESDAY)

Hearing a chopper down at the airstrip around 6:30 am, I momentarily feared it was here for me. There was no need for alarm, though; it was Mr Lovai, the headmaster, returning and what a good man. A lengthy discussion later, he expressed his bitter disappointment that I had not been offered a classroom to conduct my lessons properly. In all fairness, I am a complete stranger to the village, so I completely understand Pastor Samuel's reluctance to hand the key over without the teachers present. The diversity of my lessons made them flexible enough to teach anywhere without restricting learning to the classroom. As a result, the kids comprehended and retained English from my vocabulary and grammar games, which was the entire point.

By 8:30 am, I had shown Mr Lovai various exercises I had designed, triggering a keen interest to investigate more of this unconventional learning after my first classes. The students and I recapped yesterday's activities, then continued with a safari quiz to identify different animals and their features in the lead-up to making their own unique animals.

It was a lot of fun for the kids who hadn't encountered such a strange concept, and after a gradual start, the kids found traction, delivering some excellent results. The word of the day from that game was Guru's *camouflage,* a champion answer. I see his hope to fulfil his dreams.

To set an example for them to follow, I designed my childhood nemesis, the *Ichigooma* (thanks to Russ' brotherly teasing when we were kids), and of course, it eats little girls, which the class thought immensely funny. They all had some fun with it anyway and came up with some creative and unusual animals of their own.

After a break, the word was out that a Bird of Paradise had been caught, causing quite a bit of excitement for a while. The brilliant plumage will be used in headdresses and decorations. This particular bird was the same as one I had seen in a recent David Attenborough documentary; strikingly bright red and yellow with black eyes.

Settling back down to work on puzzles and activities using the same flashcards, the teams intermingled with younger and older students, responded well, locating all the words and checking each other's answers. A studious atmosphere descended upon the classroom as the older students engaged with younger ones like family, the whole concept proving thoroughly enthralling.

Introducing them to the *True or False* game proved a fast favourite, followed by our word game from yesterday, making as many anagrams from a single word; today's word was *tremendous*. Guru's winning team came up with 85 words.

During this industrious effort, Pastor Samuel returned to watch, either very impressed or shocked - I'm not sure which. These kids are unlocking *all* this knowledge they have stored within them, unaware I am watching them surprise themselves as much as anyone.

Mr Lovai and I had a very productive discussion after dinner, and he listened with great interest as I explained my activities and their focus points. This was all new to him, but their intriguing concept to stimulate memory retention was what he really liked. We discussed sponsorship for solar equipment in the hope of running a school computer eventually and other school necessities, which I will endeavour to obtain through Kelly's contacts.

In a spare half hour, I boxed up a few supplies for Alice and took them down to her as there were plenty left over to share amongst her family and the Lovais. Her garden is flourishing from the abundant storms and rain, so there will be a bounty of produce on her table in mere weeks. Tomorrow morning they will meet me down at the airstrip to see me off, and it will be a sad day. I'm going to miss them terribly, but the precious memories I have made will live with me. I imagine how grown my students will be when I see them next, although some will be working on the Track or have left for the city by then.

Later into the evening, while I packed my gear, Vella confidently spent an hour working on time activities for me. He's nailed it, and I'm so proud of him.

04 MAY 2017 (THURSDAY)

Breakfast at 5:00 am, and soon my remaining items were packed and ready for the chopper's arrival at 6:30 am. The boys, Nani, Caleb and I walked down past Alice's house to discover Claira and Janette were there, too, so all 11 of us headed down to the airstrip together. More joined us, including Mr Lovai and the Chief, an observant and quiet man like his brother, Barnabas, and similar in build.

Photos were taken everywhere; Alice, the Lovai's, Pastor Samuel, Ronnie, Josephine, Marie-Claire, and Freddie with his bandaged leg sporting nine stitches following yesterday's accident with a machete after school; they were all there.

Wade was my chopper pilot, once again, only this time I was the sole passenger. Stopping briefly at Kagi, we proceeded to Port Moresby, where Saii picked me up from the airport in a taxi before dropping me off at the Holiday Inn Express. As it was still quite early, my room wasn't ready, so I enjoyed some breakfast from the buffet and two amazing coffees while

I waited, which wasn't long; 10:30 am. I wasted no time. I was in there washing my hair in a long, hot shower...and yes, I can't deny it, it was blissfully good!

Sorting out my pack, I re-organised everything ready for the airport tomorrow as I reflected on many heartfelt moments. Time plays its own tricks with your senses. Just when you feel two weeks is a reasonable timespan, you quickly discover how fleeting it actually is, its swift end provoking me once again to stay as always.

Saii called in briefly downstairs around 5:00 pm, and we had a lengthy discussion about how everything went. He was genuinely interested in my progress with the kids and keen for my return so I can teach the kids in Manari Village, where his mother still lives. Manari is my next trip.

I went on to tell Saii that James Enage of the Kokoda Track Authority had called in to see me and given me his card on his way down to the chopper the other day. The inroads I had made through Pastor Samuel were also a talking point, and he enjoyed everything I had to tell him. He was very pleased all round, even though there hadn't been a classroom until the last two days, but what does that matter? When it comes down to it, these teachers are some of the most resourceful people I could ever know. They're against *all* the odds...isolation, lack of resources, exceedingly few books, and relying on the bare basics such as stones, shells, bark and whatever else they can find to simply teach these kids. Their endurance inspires me.

Eventually, I had to return to my waiting messages and emails, but with a farewell promise to Saii that we would organise my Manari trip when circumstances permit. His support has made living this dream and bonding with these wonderful people a reality; a true gift. My donation towards the Manari School will help provide classroom supplies or anything else the school might need, and he gratefully accepted my spare activities, which will support the teachers' classes.

And so, having taken care of any last details and enjoyed my last Holiday Inn Express pizza for a while, I will endeavour to get some sleep for the last time in PNG for who knows how long.

Shortly after this 2017 trip, I supplied four boxes of children's library books provided by Bundaberg Regional Library, with delivery to Efogi, Manari, Kagi and Bisiatabu Primary Schools kindly arranged by Dr Genevieve Nelson of the Kokoda Track Foundation (KTF).

My sincere thanks to the Bundaberg Regional Library and Kokoda Track Foundation for their continuing support of PNG's schools, often isolated in these remote regions.

Kelly Gatt's contacts were Mark and Julie Capper of Trek 4 Education Kokoda (T4EK), who were raising funds to assist the Kokoda Track schools but are presently restricted.

* * *

Overlooking Efogi from Launanumu. From left to right
Wilma, Marie-Claire, Vella and Guru. 2017

With Josephine, Ronnie and Guru at Efogi Creek 2017.

Sandy and Newton, Port Moresby 2017.
Photograph courtesy of Sandy Munro.

Kelly Gatt with local children along the Kokoda Track 2017.
Photograph courtesy of Kelly Gatt.

Left to right Vella, Claire Guru, Geua, Malokai (back), Jeff, Barnabas Jack (front), Freddie, Wilma, Robin. Efogi 2017.

Some of the farewell party at Efogi Airstrip, 2017.

Anzac Day Dawn Service, Brigade Hill along the Kokoda Track 2017.

Chapter 4

Edevu 2018

EDEVU PRIMARY SCHOOL - 20 July to 5 August 2018

For 12 years, my builder uncle and matron aunty made PNG's North Coast city of Lae and the Central Highland's Chimbu Province capital, Kundiawa, their home until political instability in 1967 brought them to a difficult decision; they and their 18-month-old daughter had to leave.

Yet those rugged mountains and the easy PNG lifestyle still fill them with longing 51 years later, a yearning I relate to.

Our absorbing conversations are filled with PNG stories when we get together, the reminiscence igniting happiness in their eyes and, with it, an allure of its own.

Stories from this trip would be no exception.

BRISBANE TO PORT MORESBY - 20 July 2018 (Friday)

Air traffic congestion brought a minor delay on take-off, but a good flight nonetheless, providing the ideal opportunity to revise my Motu, the vernacular of the Papuan Highlands. What I lack in practising this fascinating language, I make up for by enthusiastically increasing my Motu vocabulary.

Rewriting the detailed grammar into a convenient make-shift manual, including a Motu-English/English-Motu dictionary, is proving immeasurably valuable to my learning, enhanced further by an adaptation of my Vocabulary Board Game into Motu to assist my retention. Presently, my vocabulary equates to around 200 words, demonstrating the effective technique.

Subsequently, the late take-off meant a late arrival in Port Moresby, but Customs and Baggage Collection soon had me processed and on my way to the Holiday Inn Express shuttle. Once again, the view of these incredible mountains reaches into my heart as I look out from the 8th floor. When I see them from this end, I think of Sogeri, the popular and busy village I am yet to visit in this captivating part of the mountains nearest to Port Moresby.

As always, my dependable friend and ever-ready support, Saii Faole, has arranged this busy trip to Manari Primary School and will meet with me later to discuss the itinerary. In the meantime, my entire pack took a reshuffle, making everything easier to find before I cast an analytical eye over my informal syllabus...more of a relaxed table of sorts. Sufficient customised activities fill my lesson plans, and I am confident the students will be delighted with their results. I know I will be. Nothing is hard and fast, just effective, engrossing classes flowing at their pace.

It should all go well.

PORT MORESBY - 21 July 2018 (Saturday)

So, there is a slight change to my plans. This is what's happening now...

Choppers aren't travelling to Manari or highland villages temporarily except for specific charters, so Saii has arranged for me to travel to Edevu Village instead. He has family there, and the Seventh Day Adventist village will be perfectly safe. Edevu is only an hour from Moresby, and Saii has organised a driver to take me there with him to introduce me.

During our re-organising, Saii told me the tragic news that Ladiva, my porter from 2013, died from heart problems two months ago, in May. Apparently, he was admitted to hospital but couldn't be saved, the young, gentle carrier with a kind soul dying shortly after.

Death among younger people is a harsh reality of life here in PNG, but that doesn't make this terrible news any less shocking. It is at a time like this that you feel blessed for sharing life with those who make the world a better place.

Saii is obtaining further supplies, and I'm staying in the dependable Holiday Inn Express once again. Edevu is chilly at the moment, but other than that, I don't know what to expect, only that it's safe.

I took some time to collate my two-week syllabus and lesson plans into an instruction guide for the teachers and headmaster with easy-to-follow explanations should they wish to implement these styles in their curriculum. Learning is a beautiful thing channelled through abundant and intriguing strategies, no matter how obscure.

After messaging home to let them know about the change in my itinerary, I took the opportunity to do some washing when I showered; convenient and quick. I didn't bring my book this time and have done as much Motu as I can manage for now, so my plan is an early night. That is, if I can sleep wired with all this tingling energy.

Simply being here again with these great prospects is miraculous, and my extraordinary dream continues.

PORT MORESBY TO EDEVU - 22 July 2018 (Sunday)

Saii collected me at about 9:45 am, loading my supplies and Black Wolf pack into the ten-seater minibus before we headed off to buy the necessary groceries. All my breakfast stores were on board, saving all the usual gear; packets of my favourite mashed potato flakes, Migoreng Noodles, coconut milk powder, tinned curried chicken, tinned beef, peas, dried biscuits and milo; for this morning's shopping adventure. Not a bad spend, really, at PNGK171.34 (roughly AU$85).

Almost an hour later, the tired bitumen road leading out of Moresby brought us to Edevu's turn-off, a well-used dirt road potholed with incessant ruts and turrets typical of PNG's roadways, but Benjamin was a great driver, managing to avoid any dramas. It was a hot trip, even for Winter, and Edevu's Sunday soccer and rugby league matches were in full swing as we passed the football grounds on the village's outskirts.

Arriving at Edevu School just after 1 pm, Saii introduced me to Max Barnaba, the Headmaster, who is also Barnabas Omi's uncle. Barna was named after him, and they are unmistakably related, having the same height and build, only bearing slightly different features. Like Barna, he too possesses a thoughtful and wise nature, a gift for an immensely responsible role.

Eileen, Lema, Tau, Ester (Tau's younger sister), Bernadine and her husband Charlie, all teachers except Ester, who is a Grade 8 student, greeted me with the warmest welcome. Everyone is so kind-hearted.

Saii ensured my supplies and arrangements were all in order and returns Thursday for a brief visit to his family, as well as to check in with me that everything is going smoothly. I can reach him if necessary, and likewise, he can pass on any messages to me if there is an emergency at home.

As always, Saii has come through, with this momentous trip only possible due to his unfailing commitment.

Edevu Primary School, dominating the far side of the parade ground, is a modern two-storey building a short distance from the school village and surprisingly larger than I expected. Its long verandah fitted with steps at each end reminds me of my old Redcliffe High School Grades 9-10 block, where our Business Principal classes were held, making Edevu Primary so much more contemporary than I imagined.

Teachers across the different grades will sit in on their respective classes during my lessons, including Tau Maleva, a first-year teacher with a keen interest in my activities and the students' anticipated responses. Also fascinated by my knowledge of Motu, Tau enjoyed scanning through my compilation of the language, asking many in-depth questions with growing surprise. The printed detail was unique.

I'm solo in my teachers' quarters, with Tau and Ester rooming alongside on my right, as well as someone else on my left I am yet to meet. Everyone is so very helpful. Lema and a few others brought me firewood, some boiled water, an ample plastic container to store packet goods, a bunch of my favourite bananas, and Tau brought another thermos of hot water.

And I have a bed! Its timber platform stands about 450mm off the floor, and my self-inflating mattress fits nicely on it. Woven mats are centred on the wooden floor, and two pots of artificial purple and white orchids adorn the three tables spread with colourful tablecloths. These beautiful-hearted people have welcomed me, a complete stranger amongst them, into their lives, the privilege leaving me with such a sense of thanks I can't begin to describe.

Tau also provided some water for a shower in the back corner hut at around 4:30 pm, the freshness bringing that delicious relief after the long day's heat. While I was there, I took this perfect opportunity to do my laundry, ready to hang out along the verandah clothesline like a local and establish an early routine. I had even been provided with pegs.

Adrenalin buzzing through my already excited system played tricks on my metabolism, causing me to entirely overlook food until now. So preparing some packet mashed potato, I enjoyed my favourite PNG meal with peas, pork meat and peanuts...just what I needed.

The fact that I'm actually eating meat after being primarily vegetarian for the past 18 months doesn't matter right now. I don't wear *vegetarian* like a badge but am undertaking the alternative more as an experiment, exploring the difference a meat-free diet has on my inherent Polycystic Kidneys. One particular improvement is that great toxin-free feeling, combined with my much-improved kidney function (or GFR, to be precise). All I know is it works for me.

Interestingly, I discovered on the way from Moresby that the Nauro River runs through here from Nauro, the place full of my fondest memories where the porters sang to the grey dawn on my first trip...living memories.

And on that note, it is 9:06 pm; I will sleep well tonight.

PNG REMEMBRANCE DAY - 23 July 2018 (Monday)

Today is a public holiday to honour PNG's brave World War 2 fallen, including the Australian soldiers lying in Bomana Cemetary and unknown graves scattered throughout this remote wilderness. A blessing was held in every PNG church earlier this morning, commemorating their memory.

Almost all Papuans I know or have met are directly connected to the courageous carriers and PNG soldiers who served their country during World War 2. This is their day.

A fairly sleepless night last night, so I listened to the nocturnal birdlife, wondering what birds were making which calls, until finally drifting off to sleep around 4:30 am as the cooler night air transformed into the fresh dawn.

Unrecognisable to me, PNG is experiencing its driest time of the year. Zero rainfall with infrequent cloud cover over bare, dusty ground brings a strange sensation - almost foreign. The water tank over at the school is almost empty, and I am warned to purify the water with my Aquatabs before drinking it. Alternatively, I can always fill up Track-style from the river a few minutes away below the school...perfect.

Tau's thermos of hot water enabled me to make my morning coffee which I happily took with me to the covered assembly area to enjoy the morning. Trees and hills surround the school, making this assembly hut peacefully scenic and already my favourite place here, although I wasn't alone for long.

Joining me in their favourite place, also, were Jeremy, John and Mark, some of the Grade 8 boys who walked up from the village. They came over to say hello, and soon there was a group of eight asking enlightening questions, their interest prompted in the activities planned for them, particularly the board games. These new games had the boys curious, sparking an eagerness to try them.

Intrigued, they soon sought more, so after the Australia, Motu and Vowels Games, I tried them on the Driving Board Game, which was quite a bit of fun, too, including phonics and grammar. In what almost seemed like no time, they were regrettably heading off to a study session, returning briefly for another two games, and then home to their village.

Tau brought me a delicious lunch of curried bananas in coconut milk, a recipe I must try at home. With free time on our hands after lunch, Tau, Ester, and I went down to the Nauro River for a glorious swim, the water being swift and smooth but shallow, like Goldie River.

Ester washed the big cooking pots Tau had used for the curried bananas, politely declining any help, before finally making our way home to string our wet clothes along the veranda and generally relax. Tau explained there is a briefing tomorrow morning before class, but I won't need to arrive until after the mock exams at 10:30 am.

It doesn't seem as hot as yesterday, but the air is thick with dust and smoke from bushfires; no rain or storms in sight. Again, not much sleep.

24 July 2018 (Tuesday)

There was a peaceful quiet throughout the village as I sat enjoying my coffee in the kitchen. The early bells had sounded for in-house worship, and no one stirred outside. Through my staggered night's sleep, I'd listened to a familiar call amalgamating the stacattoed chatter of a glossy, black Spangled Drongo with the brief raucous finish similar to a Kookaburra's...that elusive Bird of Paradise. Many of the various species found here are very alike our Australian wildlife, only with slight differences in their calls or mannerisms. There is a placid, medium-sized dog everyone is fond of here in the village, and he belongs to Lema's family. An orange breed seen so often up here, he is also very well known to us in Australia, our own native dingo.

Gravitating to my favourite place in the assembly area after my morning coffee, I talked for a while with a couple from the village, when we were soon joined by Saii's brother and his wife visiting from Manari, who happily spent time getting to know me. They will stay until Sunday while Saii is here (Thursday to Sunday), and Ian, their son, will be in one of my younger classes, so I look forward to meeting him.

My 11:30 am class was the combined Grades 7 and 8, following the Seniors' practice exams, and our lesson unintentionally overran, a total lesson time of 1 1/2 hours, to be truthful. My approach was comparably bizarre to their routine, causing them to be a little unsure of just what to make of me, but it wasn't long before my activities were generating that unique atmosphere the students respond to so well. The Safari Game, with its various animals, puzzles and animal creation activity that I introduced to my Efogi students last year, once again brought similar enthusiastic responses and results; the kids loved this new learning.

This was expected to be my only class today until being asked to work with Grades 5, 6 and 7s, resulting in another resounding success. As an unorthodox ice-breaker, I introduced them to the Motu board game, an exciting activity providing common ground between us as the kids aren't overly familiar with the language, and as a consequence, it is sadly dying out. It comes as no surprise to me that the kids speak three languages; the universal Pidgin, their mother tongue and English. What humbles me is the intelligence they possess to accomplish such varied dialects, regardless of being born into such a language-diverse environment. These gifted and unassuming people are among the most articulate I have met.

Working in three teams, three students from each group happily took turns on their board, changing players at the end of each game considerately and demonstrating the most perfect manners. Not one impatient word was spoken between them, only polite cooperation; it was an absolute joy to be a part of such a bonded class.

Finishing at 3:00 pm, I came back for a shower after catching up with Eileen for a while, followed by a light tea of Saladas, vegemite and cheese. My tummy's a little ordinary after finishing Sunday's pork...it's either that or the water from the school rainwater tank.

A very light shower of rain tonight brought that sound, almost like a sigh, on the corrugated iron roof, accompanied by the divine smell of the rain wetting the earth, the petrichor. It came after tonight's hour of generator-powered lighting gave the village a reprieve to work through family activities, reading, homework and whatever the families enjoy of an evening. The petrol generator chugs away until finally spluttering to a stop, empty, and darkness returns. Efficiently timing this luxury is incredibly productive as well as social for the many families who live here.

From reports I hear, all the teachers are excited about how my lessons are progressing. There is a whole new method of teaching revealing itself before them, and each teacher is eager to see my next day's agenda.

25 July 2018 (Wednesday)

Light showers continued through the night, lulling me to sleep and relieving my dread that there might be no rain this trip. There is nothing more alien than a dusty PNG in the Dry with the very real prospect of little or no rainfall for up to four months. The thought of it just doesn't sound right, although it will at least enable the Track to dry out a little, making local travelling easier.

Coffee and a muesli bar were all I needed for breakfast before cleaning my teeth and heading over to the assembly hut to work quietly on my Motu. Before the Grade 8s finished their morning exam, Tau, Lema, Mrs Dianne Ope, and Bernadine sat with me, going through my Motu with keen interest. On showing Lema my Reverse Crossword activity completed in Motu, both she and Tau 'tested' my proficiency...well, what else would teachers do??!! There were only two I had *almost* forgotten, impressing even me.

These heartening teachers support my fresh approach and love every aspect of the learning I have brought to their school. Lema now has my email address and important information regarding some of the best grammar sites, which they should find useful, an additional boost to their extensive curriculum.

The Grade 8s had another morning exam, so I was able to take their class at 12 noon after their break. Some of the Grade 7s joined us later, so I had 28 students in total. We relocated to the unoccupied classroom next door, as there was more room on the whiteboard to work on the Make a Word Game, which was a great success, as always.

Each of my four teams (2 x Gr 7s; 2 x Gr 8s) chose the names Orchids, Kangaroos, Scorpions and Eagles, and their first word to work from was *Mathematician*. They thoroughly enjoyed themselves, frequently referring to their dictionaries to check their spelling and showing great initiative. One of the students actually chose *Dictionary* for the second word, resulting in the afternoon's triumphant winner being Orchids, with 132 words, 12 ahead of the next team. Every last one of them was positively exceptional.

Understanding their intense faith, I asked if there was anyone who might like to finish the class with a prayer, the serene and moving closure to another successful class. And so ended the day before I headed off down to the river for a longed-for swim and to top up my water. There was no one to be seen except for a few locals from the main village returning in a canoe from upriver, a thousand years captured in a moment as I watched them from the shallows.

Ester cut some firewood for me, and I made some Curried Pasta with tuna and peanuts, sharing it with Eileen, Ester and Bernadine's two children, an immensely entertaining evening for us all as we shared laughter and stories. Eventually, I was topping up my thermos from the kettle and scrubbing the pot along with anything else.

Singing down near the assembly area and the shrill of cicadas presently fill the air, the resonating sound of the insects reminding me of the 'buzz saw' cicada I heard last night, instantly transporting me back to my first trip.

Sleep Now.

26 July 2018 (Thursday)

Lema showed me three Grade 8 exam papers (Maths, English and combination), which help me identify where the students' revision is needed most. I spent time browsing through the papers, determining the activities which will assist their preparation. While I was sitting in the assembly area, Junior and a few of the other boys came over with bananas for me, which was really very kind of them

Throughout the morning, I worked with Tau's Years 3 and 4 on the Make a Word Game, enjoying the class transition from daunted to delighted as they filled the blackboard with an array of accurate words. As an extension of the exercise, I had the two teams stand back a short distance and view their opposing team's answers as we worked through them, eliminating any incorrect words and adding even more excitement to the lesson.

Listening carefully, they were totally absorbed as I explained why some of the words were incorrect due to misspellings, throwing in random antonyms or synonyms for fun. Tau watched, intrigued, as the class progressed, positively connected. This is why I am here.

A short break later, I took Years 6 and 7 for a True or False game which they loved. The atmosphere became quite competitive as all the teams play for points, but I evidently overlooked the team on the far side a couple of times when they had their hands up.

Feeling terrible on realising this, I made up for my oversight by giving them a couple of questions specifically of their own, with double points to bring them back into the game. The class agreed this was only fair, and all was soon well again.

With school over for the day, I headed down to the river to top up my water and, for sheer enjoyment, simply floated around for about 3/4 of an hour...there was nothing more relaxing. Tonight, Tau and I shared a fire, cooking some Bacon Carbonara dressed up with peanuts and some cucumber one of the teachers had given me...so good, too.

It will be a full moon tomorrow night, by the looks, that brief moment to glimpse the rising moon and setting sun on opposite horizons; nothing prettier. There must be a legend about that somewhere.

27 July 2018 (Friday)

Moonlight poured through my open window, so sleep was a long time coming until I finally drifted off near dawn for what seemed the briefest time.

Naturally, coffee was my greatest importance once I was up, so I was soon taking my steaming mug and my bleary self over to the assembly hut to enjoy the morning. Just sitting in my favourite corner, I descend into that same peaceful solitude I love so much.

Finally, my suspicions are allayed. Evidence has brought me to the conclusion that my tummy complaint was actually due to the tank water. Since drawing drinking water from the river instead and purifying it with my Aquatabs, that 'off' feeling has settled again.

This morning heralded the final exam for the Grade 8s, and on my way over to the assembly hut, one of the boys asked me if I could spend some extra lessons with him as he wanted to improve his English overall.

Of course, I gladly agreed to help. He has his future mapped out with a vision of studying to Year 12, then Uni, and completing his last year in a Malaysian University with SDA.

While waiting for the Grade 8s, we played descriptive writing and grammar board games before I tested him with the ever-proven True or False game, the hugely helpful technique enjoyed by everyone who joined us. Perfectly timed, the game ended ahead of my Years 4-5 class, another great success. Scheduled next was the combined 6-7s for an hour, followed by my Year 8s, so dividing the class into teams again, we worked on general grammar, including vowels, consonants, and syllables; a triumph and the kids loved it.

Before I started the activity, I opened the class with a photo of my son and me, talking to them about his time as a student and how his studies were not his first priority, so not the model student as perhaps supposed. The story had them captivated as I continued.

After several industrious years in a business partnership with his dad, he went on to become the successful Manager of a busy franchise, one of hundreds across Australia and New Zealand, expressing here my immense pride in my boy.

I also pointed out that, as senior students, they are far more dedicated to their lessons than he was, alight with pure interest in their classes and their futures in their faces. They thrived in that class, and a perceptible delight rippled like a current throughout the entire lesson.

Being Friday, our lesson finished early, perfect timing for my lunch of biscuits and cheese, finishing with more of that refreshing, crunchy cucumber. From the assembly hut, I could see smoke from a strategically lit bushfire near the main village drifting away from our huts on the warm afternoon breeze.

Locals had set the burn not only to clear the dense undergrowth but to chase out any game, wallabies and other small animals included, for the men to hunt in preparation for tomorrow's Sabbath.

Sundown represents the beginning of the Sabbath for the villagers, and after church on Saturday mornings, there is always fellowship among the families and villagers, with meals shared and general goodwill.

Taking in the dry, smoky and dusty hills surrounding me couldn't possibly be more opposite to my earlier trips, as the smouldering scrub appeared more Australian than the normally lush main Edevu Village I was approaching for my first real look around. Saii's brother, Allan, stopped to talk with me for a short while until we headed off in different directions, mine taking me to explore the football grounds and the local, very productive, banana plantation.

Further up the hill, I could see the sizeable community church in its prime location overlooking the village, which was the extent of my wandering before returning to the spiritual Naoro River for my reviving swim. It's no wonder the community swims twice a day; I'd be happy to stay in there all day until I turn into a prune.

After arriving back at the hut to change and string up my wet gear, I cut around to the kitchen hut to get a fire going for my Carbonara, throwing some cucumber in it and whatever else I thought might be appetising.

It was late afternoon when Saii arrived with his offsider, Tony, who comes from Alotau, an hour or so by boat to Tufi (near Popondetta). I haven't been to 'Pops', but my uncle told me a story of his time near there and how he found himself arrested for stealing a pig...yeah, don't ask.

Catching up with Saii and Tony was immensely amusing. Unfortunately for Tony, the joy of finding an article he had dropped under the hut was short-lived, thumping his head painfully against a beam. Pidgin issued forth from the darkness, and Saii's sympathetic consolation involving *bonkum narna* (translated as *bonked your head*) brought a few weak laughs from poor Tony.

Saii then continued to listen with keen interest as I explained how my classes were progressing and how wonderful this experience has been so far.

There was enough Carbonara to share between the three of us ahead of a relaxing evening with some laughs around the fire; truly perfect.

28 July 2018 (Saturday)

The bells tolled at intervals to prepare everyone for Church (except me), so there was a steady movement of people heading down to the river to wash. It is a different style of community here to Efogi, where everyone heads straight up to Church, which is both interesting and unexpected to see.

I attempted to mash up banana and Weetbix on Saii and Tony's suggestion but handed it over to Saii as it was his recipe, adding other things such as coconut milk powder, sugar and a little water creating a wonderful breakfast. It was even better than my favourite with butter and jam and definitely the polar opposite of the unappetising weetbix hydrated with hot water I endured as a kid. It kept me fed, though.

Before long, they followed the others down to the river to wash, then swam upstream to the village while I caught up on some lesson activities for the next week. Inspired by the quiet surrounding me in the empty village, I, too, headed down to the river just to sit peacefully, absorbing its beauty.

Later in the afternoon, Ester was tattooing her nickname on her forearm particularly well, using a rechargeable tattoo gun, and I immediately decided she had to tattoo a tribal harpoon design on the outside of my left hand. Drawing the design for her was fairly simple, and she liked the wording equally as much as I did; *si-aia-gu,* meaning *send me*. The tattoo gun would need to be recharged by solar, so Ester will arrange a time with me before I leave.

I made a lunch of biscuits and vegemite washed down with tomato Cup-a-Soup before settling down to read in my favourite cool spot over at the assembly hut when Nelson, a Landowner from Edevu Village, brought Eileen back from Moresby. We were talking for a little while, and he promised to take me to see the recent dam site earthworks for the new Edevu 50MW Hydro Power Station, now in its early beginnings.

China has pumped over PNG K600M (approx. AUD $260m) into the dam, a crucial project that will provide thousands of jobs and supply approximately 40% of power to the Port Moresby region in the transition to renewable energy. It will take several years to complete, but right now, it brings a palpable atmosphere of promise and excitement.

Once again, the river compelled me, and I headed down to wash, returning an hour later to start a fire and cook a pasta dinner of lentils and tomato base sauce with veges for the three of us. Probably not quite the meal they anticipated, but still flavourful.

Later, Saii and Tony talked more about the customs here in PNG and some of its everyday politics until around 10:30 p.m.

29 July 2018 (Sunday)

Today's football matches were scheduled for 8:00 a.m., but true to *Island Time*, kick-off was cheerfully lauded at almost 11:00 a.m. Many of my students were there and came to say hello, excited that I had come to enjoy the games.

Very quickly, I found myself warmly ushered to sit with some of their families, making me feel such a part of the community. I've always felt truly safe wherever I have shared the lives of PNG's kind people, and here in Edevu brings me that same enveloping feeling of being home.

Naturally, I stood out in the crowd, so it was no surprise that Saii spotted me from miles away, or at least from the other end of the pitch. Sending someone down to collect me,

I apologetically relinquished my seat with my students and their families to make my way through the crowd to his group, where we watched the games for most of the afternoon.

Someone also found two chairs for us, a totally unexpected surprise, although my protests that I was very happy to sit on the ground were dismissed with an assuring smile and a wave of Saii's hand.

There were alternate games of touch football and soccer, with women's teams sharing the agenda, making it a vigorous afternoon with some great players among them. One of them was Allan, a nimble and swift touch player cleverly doubling as a referee. As exciting as the games were, it was in the back of my mind that I was to meet Nelson at 4:00 pm. Saii had discussed the tour around the Hydro dam site with him, so it was definitely happening, but also getting late.

Eventually, with the thought crossing my mind that Nelson may have forgotten, I resigned myself to missing out on touring the project after all and considered heading back to the school when the lighthearted man arrived in his troop carrier. At the same time, a car arrived to pick up Saii and Tony for their return to Moresby, and I would see them again Thursday lunchtime when they collect me for my own return to the city.

Accompanying Nelson were his son and daughter, who are both in my classes, his son being the Grade 8 student who asked me for extra assistance. I was in good company traversing the well-worn gravel road wound through the picturesque valley, past a huge garden area belonging to nearby Binaga Village, which is home to some of my students who walk an hour to attend school. Although the village will be safe when the dam floods the valley, their life-giving garden will be lost.

This is barely the start of the Hydro project. Work begins in September 2018 and will render the valley unrecognisable upon its completion. If I don't see the finished dam, then the valley will remain forever pristine in my mind, its stunning scenery and wildlife at the heart of this memorable day, but the jobs and resources the project brings are undeniably vital to the area and a crucial step ahead for all the communities throughout the Port Moresby region. The immense benefits are life-changing.

Nearing Edevu, we pulled alongside Saii's car, where his driver had stopped at the junction, and I thanked Saii again for everything he has done to get me here before we all headed off in our own directions once again; me to cool off with another joyous swim. Naoro River's absorbing quiet remained unbroken as two women in a long canoe, a *lagatoi* loaded with bananas and river greens, poled their way downriver to the village. The long poles they used were simply extensions of themselves, as the masterful technique came so easily to them. I don't think I have ever felt so peaceful than in that moment watching them pass. There is a soul to this river, a magic that has etched its own living current into my life.

Early evening was spent cooking tea with Eileen and Lexie, my gentle neighbour from the hut on my right, and in our conversation, I discovered *musky* means *don't worry about it* or *forget it*, intriguing me so much that the thought of it makes me smile every time.

Contentment...I am immersed in it here in Edevu.

30 July 2018 (Monday)

Sleep actually came readily to me, and I managed a few hours for a nice change. Waking at dawn before the bells, I decided it was time for coffee and cucumber, and once organised for the morning, I watched the assembly of blue-uniformed students dutifully undertaking instructions. Led by Headmaster Max, the assembly began with worship, some left/right turn practice, and general advice about the dry spell currently being experienced, followed by the PNG National Anthem, passionately sung as always.

There are no more exams, so I taught Grades 7 and 8 for 1 1/2 hours, resulting in another resounding success focused on listening and speaking. Tell me my notion is wrong, but Australian history brought out some of the most exciting responses I could possibly have imagined. The teams were alive!! The kids were positively on fire with their comprehension and loved every electrifying minute!

I included Australia's doomed Z-Force Commandos who were beheaded by the Japanese in 1945 after bombing Japanese warships in Singapore Harbour; World War 1's disastrous ANZAC landing at Gallipoli in 1915; the true story of *The Rabbit Proof Fence*, and Australia's convict penal colonies of Port Arthur (Tasmania) and Norfolk Island, the ruins of their notorious 4 ft x 4 ft prison cells bearing testimony to British cruelty inflicted on their own.

Lessons with Years 5 and 6 applied articles *a/an* and *the/the* to words beginning with vowel sounds. This is always fun as not all consonants begin with consonant sounds, but more interestingly, vowel sounds. (*F*, for example, starts with an *E* sound). Then came the silent *h* in the words *hour* and *honour*, identifying another word range beginning with the vowel sound of *o*, a tricky concept that they confidently understood.

To identify long and short vowel sounds, I introduced them to the macron and the brevé, giving the lessons a more engineered connection. Again, these students are totally engrossed in everything I put to them and so very responsive. I took a class photo in all their excitement; they were just loving it all.

After stopping for an hour's lunch, it was then the Years 3 and 4's turn, working together in teams on vocabulary and listing as many descriptive words for shapes, colours and sounds as they could summon. The teams then wrote their adjectives and nouns into reverse crosswords on the board, an activity entirely new and curious to them, with their creativity quickly absorbing them.

We worked from 1 - 2:30 pm, and the kids did not want to leave (perhaps because there was a kids' working bee waiting for them!), but we'll continue the activity tomorrow. I took another class photo, and Allan's son, Ian, being shorter than many of the others, stood in front with his bilum across his chest. They all did their adorable *action* moves with their hands, then left me to attend to their tasks.

Junior and the boys were rebuilding our verandah's far stairs, cutting out the side stringers for the new treads, and I would have loved to have helped them. I would only have been intruding, though, as they were completely zoned in their work, a talent that came so naturally to them. I was happy just watching them.

This afternoon's spare time presented an ideal opportunity to gather my kitchen tablecloths and take them down to the river for a good scrub on the rocks where Eileen and Lexie do their washing. Once finished, those sheltering, cool trees were my only company as I washed my hair and swam beneath their weeping foliage.

The whole afternoon was cruisy like that, and I made some 'Deb' mashed potato with cucumber, Okari nut, yam (kau kau), kaema and peanuts, which I shared with Lexie and Tau when they returned from the river. It was as simple as boiling the kettle over the fire, so no scrubbing any smoke off pots. Convenience is king, so I'll stick with that plan for the next two nights, I think...job done.

31 July 2018 (Tuesday)

Assembly this morning was swapped for worship and hymns, and of course, the most exquisite singing hung in the air throughout Edevu Primary School as I listened from the assembly hut. Nearby in her own hut, Eileen sang in harmony with the students, unaware that her melodic voice blending with the students' had me totally transfixed.

On cue, as they finished at 8:30 am, I headed up to the Years 7 and 8s, where we started off the lesson by recapping their comprehension. True to form, their comprehension was spot on. Unsurprisingly, they'd absorbed and understood an impressive volume of information, proudly demonstrating their mastery of English skills.

This morning's lesson brought contractions and possessive pronouns into the spotlight, incorporating possessive pronouns not having apostrophes, and finished off with a blinder of a True or False game complete with its earth-shattering tight result. A palpable energy from the sheer competition filled every inch of the classroom.

Before leaving for the 10:00 am morning break, I took photos of the kids, whereupon they returned whatever desks and chairs belonged to the other classroom. No task I have asked of them has been left incomplete by any one of these respectful and cooperative students. They do their school and families proud, and I am grateful to be a part of this diligent school in the little time I have here.

Precisely at 10:30 am, Years 5 and 6 greeted me happily, and we were soon revising their a/an, the/the, and macrons/brevés, which they demonstrated beautifully. It was such a pleasure, and we then went on to recap some vowel and consonant activities, including *y*'s isolated diversity to act as both vowel and consonant.

We had enough time to include the Mountains Find a Word puzzle and an exciting Q&A activity with individual team points stretching as far as five and ten points, making proceedings *really* interesting. This exercise reviewed their comprehension of the historical theme and geography of the different mountains in the puzzle, yet another outstanding response, resulting in them all vying passionately for every point.

During our lunch break from 12 noon - 1:00 pm, I was asked to attend an unscheduled Staff Meeting at 2:00 pm this afternoon, so I was mindful of finishing my next class with the Years 3 and 4 on time.

As promised at the end of yesterday's lesson, we returned to our Reverse Crosswords, expanding on any further adjectives and nouns they were eager to add and going through any new words. The kids launched straight into their exercises, their enthusiasm giving way to concentration as the teams, Parrots, Eagles and Tigers, worked industriously to outdo each other.

Some of the new colours they learned were *burgundy, mauve, violet* and *cream*, in addition to shapes that some of the older Year 4 students acquired from textbooks; trapezium and rhombus, for instance...they truly stepped up to the challenge.

Sounds described included the explosion of a gunshot, the roar of a tiger, the revs of a truck, and so many others...simply a remarkable effort. Watching their expressions was priceless as the kids saw their Reverse Crosswords take shape, the whole concept intriguing them. Eventually, there were no more descriptions they could add, and they stood back with immense pride to admire their work. And so did I.

Gathering my delighted students, I took another photo of them in front of their impressive work, and they were all smiles. It could not have been a happier day.

I arranged with them that we'd spend more time on Motu questions from the board game tomorrow, as they were fascinated that I had put importance on demonstrating the dying language using this technique. Ultimately, the activity broadens their experience and the dialect, so a win-win for everyone.

Finishing the lesson at 2:00 pm, I headed over to the Year 5's classroom to meet with the other teachers ahead of the meeting. Bernadine and I talked about the meeting's agenda, and I was taken completely by surprise to learn I was to train them all in my techniques so they can continue my work after I return home. I was genuinely shocked, explaining that the kids all had the knowledge inside their heads and that the teachers are doing a commendable job; just keep doing what they are already doing because it is working.

Ultimately though, my techniques unlock their knowledge as they compete for points, creating energy that, although unorthodox, is an effective alternative to the traditional copying from the blackboard. I further explained that the activities I use are great for revision or reviewing the students' progress and especially useful in the lead-up to exams, such as those the Year 8s face in October.

I also defined Word Ladders, Vowel Flowers, Draw the Teacher (instead of points), my customised True or False Game and Reverse Crossword technique, a great tool that I had been using with Years 3 and 4 over the past two days with a twist on phonics and effective vocabulary building.

Extending these exercises further, I explained my descriptive writing activities for Years 7 and 8 and their focus on the stimulating use of adverbs and adjectives to join shorter sentences, making for more interesting reading.

These were the activities I had compiled into a guide specifically to leave for them, important now more than ever with the imminent exams foremost in everyone's minds.

Everything was so well received, and plenty was being noted, especially by Headmaster Max. The meeting concluded a little over half an hour later, with their gratitude, and I headed off to check on a few things before taking my water bottle down to the river.

As planned, I made a simple dinner of mashed potato with cucumber, pork and peanuts by boiling water over the fire in the kitchen hut; quick, simple and clean. My last tasks were topping up my thermos for my morning coffee and washing up.

Shortly after Max had started the community's revered generator, Tau and Bernadine came over for a long chat, and we exchanged email addresses, as well as my phone number and postal address. We had a lot of laughs and generally just had an easy, relaxed time together. The generator is off now, and my Edevu sisters have gone back to their homes, albeit Tau is next door, so I am heading off to bed.

Grasshoppers! Two have just come through my window, attracted by my headlamp...but not for long.

01/08/2018 (Wednesday)

First day of August...where is the year going?!

Activity buzzed around the village this morning, ahead of what I understand is a P&C Meeting at 2:00 pm this afternoon. Organised for the morning, I took myself contentedly over to my Years 7 and 8, discovering even more stirring as chairs were positioned in front of the school.

They were setting up for a complete school photo of all primary grades and their teachers (me included), with a framed enlargement intended for me as a thank-you gift. Lema had to tell me in case the gift would be compromised going through Customs on my return to Australia.

Still totally astonished, I suggested that the glass in the photo frame might be an issue, either by breaking in my pack or being confiscated before boarding, so she will have the photograph laminated for me instead, the perfect solution.

She also asked about bilums and anything wooden etc., so I told her what I knew; bilums are permitted, but wooden items could be dodgy, although the wooden souvenirs carved by the trekkers' porters make it through customs alright.

Taking Years 7 and 8, we recapped on Z-Force and other comprehension lessons from yesterday before embarking on contractions and other revision they would need to assist them in preparing for their exams. With 20 minutes remaining, I gave the class free rein to select their own main words for their favourite word game, and they were all just on fire. Each of the two teams identified over 110 words, even if we did overrun by 30 minutes. I wasn't going to stop them - they were loving it, and it was no inconvenience to anyone.

Years 5 and 6 were next, revising vowels and consonants, silent letters and articles a/an and the/the complete with macrons and brevés; another sweeping success. What great kids - they simply love learning. I introduced them to Vowel Flowers, then let them loose at the board. The teams allocated their own vowel for the flower's centre, and whichever consonants they chose for each petal, and once again, they had the greatest fun making as many words as their teams could find.

With the activity rapidly escalating into another fast favourite, the teams wanted more. This was when they met the challenge of double vowels with the same number of consonants for an even more impressive result. Sitting in on the class, Bernadine loved what she saw, and while the kids worked, I showed her the Word Ladders I had prepared, demonstrating their structure and how the activity built the students' vocabulary. Its creativity intrigued her, and she loved the concept.

Finishing on time for a lunch of biscuits and vegemite washed down with a welcome coffee, I headed over to the Years 3 and 4 at 1:00 pm, where we recapped colours, shapes and sounds, applying any new words in sentences or using them as descriptive examples. Then began *their* creative journey with Vowel Flowers, which they also loved immensely; another great success.

As it turns out, I taught Grace last year at Efogi. Grace is an adorable and bright young girl who absorbs every detail and, like all the kids, applies herself to any task. Her younger sister, Sharron, and her friends were with me for quite a while this afternoon, and she told me she remembered me from Efogi. Sorrow and gratitude hit me all at once when Grace told me how much everyone missed me when I left.

I just wished she had told me much sooner that she was from Efogi, as I felt awful that I hadn't realised; there have been so many faces. Sharron is in Elementary School (Years 1 and 2), so I haven't been teaching her here, but she seemed to think I had taught her at Efogi, too; I'll have to look at my photos to make sure. Neither of them is in the class photo I have in my office, and I only had two official classes the entire time, so she may have been in the first class of 20 students. They are both sweet girls, and all their friends are lovely, too.

To my delight, Grace told me about Vella, Guru, Freddie and Claira when I asked her about them, and she also explained to me that she and her family are here until 2020. They all accompanied me down to the river so I could wash my tea towel and my hair without getting my clothes too wet, saving my wash for later.

The kids wanted to play one of the board games when we walked back, so I had them playing amongst themselves out in the kitchen while I started packing. Ester came over to tattoo my hand, but the tattoo gun ran out of charge partway through. Right now, I have a thin, sexy blue line and nothing else, but I'll get it finished back home for my birthday.

On leaving, the kids told me they will all miss me but are looking forward to our morning class tomorrow. Surrounded by a family atmosphere in that moment, we shared hugs, bringing a painful awareness of just how much I will miss them all, too.

Sadly, my last night here in Edevu has come so soon. Testimony to my careful rationing, there are still plenty of groceries for everyone to take whatever they wish for themselves as my thank-you gift. I was given another cucumber, more of my favourite bananas and a paw paw, which I won't be able to get through, but will leave for the others to enjoy with the remaining groceries. Lema and one of the students know these bananas are my favourite and also brought me some. How I wish I could take them home...their deliciousness is unequalled. Everybody is so selfless and giving, their natural kindness warming me wherever I go. These beautiful-hearted people will stay with me always, however far apart we may be.

I won't miss these grasshoppers, though. I've just removed the third one now, so I must be overcoming my dread of them...*just perhaps*. They're a different build of grasshopper, more rocket-shaped than any insect I've ever seen.

Max also stopped as he passed by to let me know that Saii had spoken to him and he will pick me up at 10 am tomorrow. Sounds like a plan...sadly, I'll be ready.

2 August 2018 (Thursday)

Being my typically organised self, I had my bed, pillow and sleeping bag all packed with everything ready to go before greeting my last class at Edevu Primary School. Lema came over early with Bernadine on behalf of the school to give me a stunning bilum that Max's wife had woven for me. Totally unexpected, I thanked them all, telling them that I have a special place for the precious gift in my PNG Room at home.

Everyone attended my class this morning, not just my 7s and 8s, and I introduced them to my poem, *Somewhere Along the Kokoda Track*.

I began by telling them the story of the last two lines haunting me from Templetons Crossing to Owers Corner, and then for the next four years until I finally sat down and wrote the rest of the poem. The entire class thought it was great, and when I came to those last two lines, I simply pointed to the words, and the students finished the poem for me. It was a poignant moment, another one I will take with me in my long list of unforgettable memories.

This morning was all about requests, and so it was they unanimously wanted their favourite, the Make a Word Game. And boy, did they what! Each team chose their nominated word and proceeded to make over 120 words from them; it did me good just watching their success unfurl. Naturally, I took photos and Eileen, who had come to watch the classroom fun, took some of the kids with me, too.

A number of students and parents surprised me with bilums, and little Ian gave me a kiapa, a broader string bag used for carrying firewood. Among them was another type similarly woven to Ladiva's bag all those years ago, from the bark of the tulip tree. These wonderful kids are all so sweet, and little Ian is right there with the best of them.

Tau knows I will endeavour to get back next year, if I can, to help the Year 8s with their exam preparations. I also promised to email more activities that they can print off for the lessons.

It was 10 am, all too soon, so I headed over to be ready at my hut for when the car arrived. In minutes I had my gear out on the veranda, ready to load up, but there was no car yet. Jeremy and Mark came over to say goodbye, also, and Eileen took photos of them with me.

My parting inspiration to them was not to be afraid of their exams as they are what will take them into their futures. Jeremy wants to be a teacher or lawyer, and Mark an engineer. I can see their futures in their eyes...it's what they want. This means I won't see them next year when I come back, as they will be either in Port Moresby or Mt Diamond High Schools, and who knows where after that.

I hope I've given them enough to help them get there.

Many of my students had come down to visit me in farewell, and as we walked over to the assembly hut to sit in the cool one last time, we discovered Saii's white four-wheel drive under a nearby tree a short distance from us.

And so, on that note, we loaded up and, with last hugs all around, headed up the dirt road past Edevu Village, slowing down briefly to talk to a guy walking alongside the track, who Saii later told me was Ladiva's brother. Eileen had caught an opportune lift to Port Moresby with us, and on my arrival at the Holiday Inn Express, I was in time to check in and enjoy a long, luxurious hot shower.

As arranged, Saii returned for pizza so we could examine details about the school's needs in my endeavour to raise sponsorship. During that conversation, we discussed the water situation, a matter of great concern to him. As a Community Leader, Saii identifies the community's greater needs and the wisest methods to resolve these issues, water clearly a priority.

I explained to him that the guttering at Edevu runs along one side of each family's roof, and the second tank at the main school was relocated to supply one of the houses, again with guttering fitted only on one side. Understanding its impact, Saii agreed that if the remaining half of each roof ran guttering to their respective tanks, no house (or the school) should run dry, especially if another tank was positioned to catch any vital runoff.

Saii's suggestion of piping water up from the river to a tap for everyone's use is arguably the most affordable solution, although the pump's security remains questionable. There will be major changes coming to the school with the hydro project bringing extra students and funding, I'm sure, but I have promised to pursue sponsorship and whatever assistance I can possibly provide.

This dedicated champion for his People headed home to his family shortly after on my assurance I would help to the best of my capacity, hopefully returning to prepare next year's Edevu Grade 8's for their October exams. as well as teach

Manari's happy children; their infectious laughter still makes me smile. They would be five years older now, but no one could be too old to enjoy that swing behind the guest house.

For now, in the afterglow of these memories, the solace of my remaining time here reaches for me on this wild yet peaceable island that keeps calling me back.

Tau Maleva and May Dehl, one of the students from my enterprising Year 8 class, both confirmed all the Grade 8s made it through to high school. My heart is full.

Tragically, three months later, Gina, a former Edevu Primary School student home for Christmas after completing Grade 9 at Mt Diamond High School, was making her way down the river bank to wash the kitchen pots and pans, when she fatally slipped, dying at the river from her injuries.

Since my return home, all my attempts to arrange sponsorship to prevent such a tragedy have been unsuccessful or gone unanswered.

* * *

Edevu Primary School, Edevu 2018

Years 7-8 class, Edevu 2018.

Years 5-6 class, Edevu 2018.

Years 3-4 class, Edevu 2018.

Teachers at Edevu Primary School. (From left to right) Lema, Tau, Bernadine, unknown, Lexie, Freda, unknown, Headmaster Max Barnabas, Charlie. Edevu 2018.

Last day of school, Edevu 2018.

Beginning of earthworks on the Edevu Hydro Project,
Edevu 2018.

Nauro River, Edevu 2018.

Chapter 5

Kokoda Track Foundation Research Project 2019

> Kokoda Track Foundation Research Trip (Kokoda to Sanananda) - 29 June to 06 July 2019

A soft quietness steals and the moonlight reveals the result of this death-dealing game,
The sky rains its dew as if all nature too were weeping with pity and shame.
An unseen hand has sketched on the sand a pattern just out of reach,
Of many a wave that flows o'er a grave on the Sanananda Beach.

Extract from On the Sanananda Beach
Pte C.R. Shaw, Q126475 (1943)

Fated to breaking my plastic camping plates as I am, I had to purchase one this morning to replace my last unfortunate casualty, broken on my way home from Edevu. Don't ask me how I do it...I just do.

This will be my first visit to PNG's North Coast schools and their teachers, a trip made all the more unique with Dr Genevieve Nelson's Kokoda Track Foundation (KTF) driving this remarkable project.

KTF's extraordinary vision delivers educational and health programs from centres throughout the remote regions of PNG, an immense source of learning for developing young futures. My role is to collect research and data from approximately 20 KTF teachers from Kokoda to Sanananda while Petra Arifea, an exceptional Program Manager and trusted colleague, works simultaneously along the Mt Hagen corridor, correlating information from its regional provinces. We won't link up, but we will be in touch through my team waiting for me at Popondetta and whenever Wi-Fi permits.

On my return home, I will compile my report for presenting to the Prime Minister, Hon. Peter O'Neill, a ground-breaking step towards these dedicated teachers attaining their teaching qualifications and recognition in the eyes of PNG's Ministry of Education, their triumph.

Let's get these teachers their long-awaited qualifications.

Brisbane to Port Moresby - 30 June 2019 (Sunday)

Touching down at Jackson Airport gave me that same *I'm home* feeling that welcomes me to Port Moresby, with a 3:00 pm shuttle waiting to take me straight to the Airways Hotel. My messages home were swiftly followed by touching base with Saii Faole and Wilma (Wilz) Mavea, my remarkable PNG *susa* (sister), who will try to meet me at the International

Airport on my way back on 5 July. Wilz is a true *pawa meri*, one of those fearless PNG women who has achieved a remarkable career through her studies, breaking barriers and overcoming all adversities to follow her dreams, as well as excelling in her role as KTF Project Coordinator.

My old friend, Saii Faole, has evolved into the powerful leader he was born to be, the Chief of Manari Village. We caught up briefly for pizza, and his devoted support of the Kokoda Track villages continues through KTF. Hearing all his news and sharing old times, including fond memories of his mum and dad, were joyous. It thrilled me to hear of the memorial being constructed at Manari to honour his dad, Faole Bokoi, the last of the Fuzzy Wuzzy Angels, his clear image wearing his medals suddenly filling my mind as if he were right there.

Progress on Manari High School has temporarily stalled at the library Barnabas built, assisted by his team of carpenters. Barna often builds houses throughout Manari for Saii during the Track's seasonal closure, the monsoonal months of October to March. And PNG does some serious *monsoonal*.

While I'm on the library subject, one of my donated boxes of children's books, graciously delivered by KTF last November, is eagerly enjoyed by Manari's school children, and there is room on its shelves for many more.

On Dr Gen's recommendation, I later arranged for Kathy Blundstone's generous delivery of children's books through Heather Doonan's Brisbane-based *Books 4 PNG Kids*, another committed volunteer-oriented group coordinated by Evelyn Jarua in PNG under the Safe School Initiative (S2CP), and the Dept of Justice & Attorney General (DJAG). Collectively, they aim to create safe learning for children in schools, focusing on strengthening respect for the rule of law through education.

This dynamic *pawa meri's* vision compelled her to launch the Liklik Tasol Stori Book Project (Little Readers Story Book Project), a further initiative of the S2CP and DJAG, not only delivering reading books to PNG's rural schools but also distributing school stationery, another learning essential in drastic short supply.

And so it begins, that same keyed anticipation. Typical of this restlessness during my PNG visits, I find it difficult to sleep, seemingly my own quirky way of spending as much time in PNG as I can.

Links:

Books 4 PNG Kids (Aust)*: books4pngkids.org/*

Books 4 PNG Kids (Port Moresby) Evelyn Jarua*: facebook.com/evelyn.jarua*

Liklik Tasol Stori Book Project:

https://uphatter.com/campaign/4789/liklik-stori-tasol-book-project?fbclid=IwAR0zTS4dzr-Lglj6LMuUFTKaDC3GZ6VSTXCpvcAxLqMs25N2fAGgrdxa0Ts

Email: *books4pngkids@gmail.com*

Port Moresby to Popondetta to Kokoda -1 July 2019 (Monday)

Sam Kaima, our Team Manager, met me at the Port Moresby Domestic Airport, Saraga, after the hotel shuttle dropped me off at 6:05 am, way ahead of schedule in all my eagerness. Sam arrived soon after, spotting me easily, not only due to my being naturally detectable but also as I was wearing the KTF shirt Petra had organised for me back in Brisbane.

Popondetta's new airport, a 35-minute flight from Port Moresby, was opened last Wednesday, and where we were warmly met by Grayson Kaumi and our driver, Clyde Arabata.

Grayson is from Sanananda Village and a loyal KTF Projects Coordinator, while Clyde is a welcoming Popondetta local who knows his way around these roads like no driver I've ever met. This is a team like no other.

With our gear loaded into the back of the Landcruiser, we headed into Popondetta, or more colloquially, *Pops*, to pick up all the usual supplies of noodles, tinned pork, powdered milk, cereal, etc., before resuming our travels under Clyde's skilled handling of the rough Gorari-Kokoda road. The road often resembled a minefield, pot-holed with water-logged craters and typically rough as guts. But we're here, it's PNG, and there is nothing better.

Stopping briefly at Gorari, we were met by the school's Head Teacher, Dorcas, who gladly accepted some of my printouts and materials to assist the school. Then on to beautiful Kokoda. Waiting for us to collect them was the maintenance crew, Joe Inoro, Theo Laimo and Selwin Suma, who were delivering cement for Kokoda College's water tanks, the task well coordinated with my afternoon interview of six incredible teachers; Patricia, Roisey, Kerry-Anne, Molly, Anne and Theresa.

Inspiring is how I define these remarkable women from today's interviews. Theresa and Roisey have been approached to write manuals to assist the Government Training Programs, while Patricia is highly esteemed for her superior phonics skills. By her own initiative, Patricia added Librarian and Grade 3 teacher to her proven abilities, ambitiously becoming Kokoda College's Projects and Welfare Officer.

The communities assist by providing the volunteer teachers with fruit and vegetables until paid employment begins. From this point, the teachers rely on their own produce, not only for themselves but to sell at the markets for purchasing any necessary classroom materials. An example of community support is Hoi School's double classroom, funded by the local councillor and built by parents from the village for Anne, their young teacher. It struck me that there had been no sign of a school at Hoi on my earlier treks, but I am eager to return to see it.

As Kou Kou's only high school student, Molly, the youngest of my devoted teachers, was directed into the pedagogy world by her community and village leader, and her instinctive talent and dedication to her students are a gift. At barely 20 years old, Molly carries her role with glowing pride, teaching prep and other eager learners in the community hall while her classroom is built.

Roisey accommodates the lack of reading supplies by artfully writing and illustrating her own stories, stapling the pages into books to provide readers to her students, her natural leadership not going unnoticed by school administrators and parents. It also comes as no surprise to learn Roisey acquires extra children to her classes, their parents depositing them assuredly into her care, then watching the classes from outside the windows to observe her teaching skills and assist her work on the home front.

Lacking the necessary resources continues to challenge them, requiring the teachers to improvise by gathering stones for counting, bark for textures, flowers for colours, vegetable peels for letters, seeds for art, etc., from their surrounding environment. Long distances for the students to attend school through monsoonal downpours, surging rivers, blistering equatorial heat, and sheer wilderness contribute to the difficulties. Older girls are encouraged to walk in groups to avoid being attacked, a very real danger that often results in pregnancies.

Welcome to their world...

Recording most of the interview to save time, the entire session took approximately 2 hours, subsequently finishing in the fading dusky light, the time to set ourselves up for the night. This was when I met the college headmaster, Enosh Ben, his wife, as well as Philip Ararai, the Community Liaison

Officer, and Amanda, a cheery trainee nurse who generously shares her hut with me tonight.

Steaming rice, cooked bananas, pumpkin tops, and a delicious stirfry of celery and meat with noodles awaited us in the college hall, a flavoursome dinner perfectly cooked by Maryanne Suma and another kind lady. Contentment glowed on everyone's faces, and fond memories of cooking over the fire at Edevu came back to me as I wondered what the kitchen facilities were like here at the College.

Whatever their arrangements, it heightens the relaxed atmosphere I love about PNG, and Kokoda transforms into an entirely unexpected psyche. No longer is it the pivotal destination of a brutal trek historically shadowed by death, but a new beginning where dreams are brought to life, the embodiment of today and tomorrow.

Kokoda to Gorari - 2 July 2019 (Tuesday)

Sleeping surprisingly soundly after drifting off to the beautiful sound of the rain, I awoke around 7:00 am to discover breakfast would be in the hall at 7:30 am and that it had continued raining the entire night. Gathering my gear and paperwork, I checked a third time, ensuring nothing was overlooked before leaving my pack inside the door. Our first visit was to call in at Kou Kou Infants, a few minutes away, to see Molly in her classroom, and I was taken by complete surprise at the school's unexpected beauty. I don't know why, really, with the school nestled in the heart of the wild Owen Stanley Range, but it did; the perfect vision of green neatness dotted serenely with thatched huts. What is there not to love?

I was disappointed for Molly that she has never received reading books, so I promised to send her children's library books as I had sent to Efogi, Manari, Kagi and Edevu Schools last year. *When* is another question, but hopefully much sooner than later.

Heading back to Kokoda, I spent more time with the warm and motherly Roisey, discussing classroom techniques and any suggestions I could recommend. More than just a colleague, Roisey and I formed a friendship in a unique moment of shared empathy. Patricia also came especially to see me at the college for a longer chat concerning many interesting factors she had held back from yesterday's discussion. Speaking more openly on her own, I was thankful for the opportunity to add her compelling merits to my notes.

This is a woman who is not only passionate about the future of teaching but a beacon for others to follow. Another true *pawa meri*, Patricia cuts a blazing trail with her vision and inexhaustible spirit, another radiant example of PNG's leaders of tomorrow.

Meeting Rolph and Benchley at Kokoda Primary, we discussed the immense benefits of technology and its influence on today's learning. This conversation not only led to technology in PNG schools but students engaging in online learning through their phones, depending on reliable signal and sufficient phone credit to engage successfully.

Returning to the college, we enjoyed Maryanne's hot lunch before thanking our hosts for their generous hospitality and Amanda for sharing her lodgings with me, then on to Gorari. A night of rain did nothing to improve road conditions, but this didn't stop us from making our way up to the Kokoda Memorial, where *Kokoda Spirit Trekking Company* had just finished their arduous journey from Owers Corner. Every expression on their drawn faces ignited sensations of exhaustion to the souls of my feet. No familiar porters, though.

This is my first visit to Gorari, where Grayson, Sam, Clyde and I are staying at Handari Village's picturesque Gorari Guesthouse as their first guests. All down the track to the lodge, we were welcomed by calls of *Oro kaiva (Welcome home)* from the proprietors, Phanuel Ambo and his generous wife.

Having settled in, we continued our drive into Gorari to meet Cornelius and Wari Pondo, a husband and wife team dedicated to teaching their young students at Gorari Primary School. Together, they have taught for seven years with another two years of study ahead. I look forward to talking more with them at tomorrow morning's interview; they have so much to tell me.

After a long day, I looked forward to my blissful swim in the river and washing my hair, so now happily go to bed on a full stomach of noodles, cooked bananas, rice and taro. There were none of my favourite choko leaves at the market today, an insignificance, really, as I listen to the night birds calling and the squealing cicadas above the river's gentle murmur.

In memory of Molly Bedi, passionate teacher of Kou Kou Infants School, Kou Kou, who touched everyone's heart. Tragically, Molly wouldn't live to see her students receive their books in 2022.

May her spirit shine for others to follow.

Gorari to Sanananda - 3 July 2019 (Wednesday)

We woke to the birds' dawn chorus, and how typical of me to feel the start of a sore throat unless I've been snoring (which I don't). Either way, I really hope not. I haven't used my sleeping bag, having slept in warm clothes instead, which seemed to be enough, or so I thought.

Uncharacteristically, I had a breakfast of chocolate cereal and milk, ideal for my low sugar levels and wonderfully matched with my coffee bags, a dependable morning staple.

Sam, Grayson and Clyde all enjoyed some light-humoured morning banter with me before taking some photos and gathering our gear, ready to leave for Gorari.

The Ambos looked after us warmly in this sweet village and allowed me to take photos of them in front of our newly built hut as were leaving. On the way, Grayson mentioned that we might be able to see Alice Ijuri, my Efogi *susa*, who I am told is now working in nearby Buna, a thought that especially thrilled me.

Setting up for the continuing interviews didn't take long, and I was soon greeting Head Teachers Cornelius and Wari Pondo. This tenacious couple is a committed team, leading the school creatively and setting the perfect example as role models. In 2014 there was no Head Teacher, so Wari and Cornelius ran the school together for one year, until Wari was left to run the school on her own while Cornelius was undertaking his 6-month Elementary Course at Kokoda College.

On his return, they continued to run the school together, relying on KTF funding as government funding was refused. The community assists by generously cleaning 16-year-old Gorari School, along with the Church maintaining the school grounds and providing Religious Instruction lessons.

A day at Gorari School begins with an outdoor assembly (Mon/Wed/Fri) and announcements, including school rules, disciplines, and songs, until finishing with group and individual activities. Importantly, girls are given equal opportunities as boys, and those with disabilities are confidently included, naturally interested in their lessons.

Cornelius and Wari adapted to teaching a Grade 2 disabled student unable to use his right hand by assisting and supporting him to write left-handed instead, a strategy introduced by the child's parents. Strengthening exercises provided better control and development of the child's left-handed skills, preparing him for writing left-handed, beginning with tracing and scribbling, another valuable tool in Cornelius and Wari's expanding experiences.

With Cornelius and Wari's interview concluded, my next group of teachers included Christy and Linda of nearby Waju Village and Gwen from Kokoda, who hadn't been advised of yesterday's interview, so made hurried arrangements to attend this morning's interview instead. What a winning bunch of ladies! They have such grit and a heart for teaching yet are denied their accreditations by the Ministry of Education; I simply can't believe the injustice. Their stories are inspirational, and every minute with them is a journey.

Linda worked in a government teaching role for 17 years, receiving her KTF training three years ago, whereas Christy is solely KTF-trained and has been a KTF volunteer for nine years. Linda particularly appreciated KTF taking their time to ensure she was on track with her learning through the course, compared to the rushed government training. She, too, looks forward to more training to teach children with disabilities as she has a deaf student and needs upskilling to better help him, cleverly adapting lessons wherever necessary.

Community support often provides food offerings Tuesdays and Thursdays as well as an infrequent PNG K2/month, although the monthly subsidy has practically discontinued. The students clean around the school yards, gardens and in the classroom with their teacher, and although parents assist with homework at home, they are deterred from assisting in the classroom to prevent them from writing for the children and taking over their work.

The school put on a splendid lunch halfway through when locals, Merolyn and Fethol from Kebara arrived to join the group. Together they shared compelling stories with me, covering all aspects of their students' needs, including those with disabilities and others who travel through difficult terrain to attend school. Their limited supplies result in the teachers using stones for counting, bark and feathers for descriptive textures, and many other creative techniques.

Linda and Christy currently volunteer under KTF, receiving community support of food contributions on Tuesdays and Thursdays, and the children clean the yards, gardens and classroom with the teacher. Following her training, Fethol was initially given a shelter to begin her classes, her own classroom built later by her community.

When Kebara Elementary School opened, Linda demonstrated her natural leadership in charge after only six weeks of training, using all materials she could locate for resources, including rubbish. Christy's students were introduced to the surprising use of pieces of concrete for counting, innovative within the school's limited means.

Their KTF training in phonics has been a great skill-builder, an aspect all the teachers optimistically agree gives them greater insight and understanding of word-building and is especially engaging in the classroom.

Merolyn is particularly proud to be part of the first intake of teachers to learn phonics, and each feels their training and skills give them greater standing and superior quality teaching than government-trained teachers. Their self-confidence enables them to bring out the best in their students, evident through an inner strength clearly obvious in their eyes as they open their world to me.

Gwen's KTF training enabled other teachers to learn the skill of making books by sewing the pages together along the spine. Resources again ranged across all textures; charcoal, clay, stones, sticks, leaves, petals, seeds and bark; implemented into their personally designed lesson plans within their training and curriculum. Merolyn particularly finds maths and phonics brings out the best connection with her students by creating fun lessons for phonics, reading and using stones for counting, the kids' familiar favourites.

Their lack of accreditation is a desperate issue, stone-walling them from achieving their dreams. Each dedicated teacher endeavours to complete their final Years 10-12 before progressing to further Diploma studies. The vision these inspirational teachers have for the future is that the PNG Government recognises their KTF training and grants their accreditations.

Once again, I ran over time, but they were all eager to share their stories, and I was equally as eager to record every word. It wasn't particularly late when we left for Sanananda, even after some photos, and Clyde masterfully negotiated the rugged, turreted road steeped in history along the way, its epitome, the fortified World War 2 Japanese bunkers.

There were approximately ten of them overgrown by Kunai Grass and positioned on both sides of the road. The area bore a remarkable resemblance to the dirt track where George Silk captured the iconic image of the temporarily blinded George (Dick) Whittington with his bandaged eyes, led by Fuzzy Wuzzy Angel, Raphael Oimbare. I wouldn't say it was the precise location, but it was awfully close to Buna.

We also crossed the one and only Wairope River earlier today, so-named for its wire rope origins during World War 2, its legendary crossing now crowded with villagers swimming and washing clothes.

This road ends at the beautiful village of Sanananda, and on our arrival at dusk, the towering palms stood silhouetted against the sunset's last light, intensifying my anticipation for tomorrow's early morning walk. Immense battles were fought through here in 1942-1943, the entire campaign beginning and ending on these local beaches, and Grayson has arranged to show me the wrecks of the Japanese landing barges tomorrow.

This is Grayson's village. He is greatly respected and introduced me to Neil Pearson, one of the teachers I am interviewing tomorrow. Neil showed us to our individual rooms and the well-built shower hut with two showers and toilets. Being height-challenged, the tap was too high for me, so one of the helpful ladies brought me a bucket of water to use instead.

The solar lights were kept alight throughout the camp, and a generator continued running a short distance away as our dinner was brought over to our open hut. Having stopped to buy fresh chicken on the way, our sensational dinner was, of course, Curried Chicken, greens, rice and bananas - exceptional. Everyone is so hearty and kind, and Neil's uncle from across the inlet visited in an outrigger, arriving with many interesting stories of the village.

By tradition, tonight finds the names of all the teachers I have interviewed written in Patrick's book, with Grayson, Sam, Clyde and Neil signing it themselves. Among these many treasured names are Dr Genevieve Nelson, Wilz and Petra, so no one is missing out, as I leave the book with Sam to enjoy reading it a little longer. What an extraordinary trip, gifted with unforgettable people and the days they shared with me.

It is around 10:00 pm. Out in the clear night air, the sound of Holnicote Bay's rolling surf carries on the gentle Sanananda breeze - how Dad would love it.

Sanananda to Popondetta - 4 July 2019 (Thursday)

What a privilege to wake up to this stunning panorama. Those huge leaning palm trees commanded their place along the inlet, overlooking the village's neatly thatched huts. People everywhere settled into their daily lives. Smoke drifted in the air, roosters crowing, pigs squealing and grunting, and all around, relaxed conversations in Pidgin hummed, dotted with that ever-amusing *aaaheee* occasionally lilting through gentle laughter. I am lost somewhere in all its charm.

With the estuary dividing the village at high tide, the crossing was rendered impossible, so Neil ferried Sam and me separately to the beach in an outrigger - positively memorable. Looking back towards the village, I watched the smoke rising lazily from kitchen fires on each side of the inlet, and in moments we were out walking along the beach.

Neil showed us the remains of three Japanese landing barges, now covered in barnacles with their rusting hulks protruding from the water, while beneath us their decaying wreckage could easily be seen in the shallow waters along the banks. This was where the final blow was struck and among some of the most intensive battles, pushing the Japanese back into the sea.

There were more barges around the corner towards Buna, and touching one of these alongside the outrigger's canoe brought visions of incomprehensible horrors endured in this peaceful place. Images came to me of Japanese uniforms and boots hurrying en-mass from the barges; real people, soldiers under orders to take this beautiful country and proceed to descend upon Australia.

On returning from our outrigger escape, breakfast and coffee were on our agenda before wandering through Sanananda's markets, where Grayson introduced me to his grandmother, Charlotte, the most beautiful-hearted *meri*. She gave me a cowrie shell necklace, a colourful bilum she had lovingly made, and no end of hugs.

Her wise eyes tell a thousand words, and Grayson explained that she and his grandfather used to dive off the landing barges as kids growing up. Imagine the polar opposite of these sleeping death machines, from feared to revered, one of their final roles rendering them fun-filled platforms for endless childhood memories, another as tourist attractions.

My remaining morning was spent interviewing Neil and Walter Ekeba, an older teacher who had made the hour's walk from Buna. Both teachers had significant differences, making my research immensely interesting, Neil being singularly KTF while Walter had been a Government teacher for six years.

Neil has 75 students (Prep and Elementary 1 and 2), and the classroom, built by the community, includes a library catering for the surrounding Sanananda population. Selected from Lower Secondary (High School), Neil attended KTF teacher training in one of Sanananda's community halls until the community built his school where he launched into his teaching career seven years ago.

Walter's community doesn't provide food supplies but assisted immeasurably by building the Buna Elementary School's double classroom for his 21 Elementary 1 and 2 students, although the school currently doesn't have a library. Walter went straight into Buna Elementary after completing his government-sponsored teacher training and has been teaching in this school for the past 19 years, 13 of them with KTF.

After Walter's government training, he compared the two and found KTF's training more wholesome, providing better knowledge and information, as well as the evaluations being a great confidence-builder. This has enabled him to build his skills effectively as an experienced teacher. Government training hadn't included early childhood or provided tasks for exploring this age group. By comparison, KTF's valuable training delivered evaluations and feedback to support his learning. Both teachers maintained that KTF trainers' mentoring prepared them with effective teaching skills, building them into the successful teachers they are today.

The Church also assists with keeping both school grounds and classrooms clean, providing Religious Instruction, assisting with reading and writing in class as part of the curriculum, and providing necessary support for both schools. It is my intense wish to see all these devoted teachers accredited; let this be the time.

Two hours later, we were enjoying a lunch of cooked bananas with rice and greens washed down with the quenching milk from a freshly opened coconut before we had to leave.

Typically, a cold has definitely taken hold, its unpleasantness easing with every cold and flu tablet I throw down. And so, with myself dosed up to the gills and the 4-wheel drive packed, we farewelled beautiful Sanananda Village and matriarch Grandma Charlotte for Popondetta, inwardly rescheduling Alice Ijuri's catch-up for another trip when there would be more time to visit Ibogo.

Clyde stopped at the Japanese airstrip on Sanananda's outskirts, especially for me to take in the history. Now a deserted airstrip, the Japanese had built this intrinsic lifeline with bulk concrete, a plentiful resource considering the number of bunkers surrounding us, bringing their grim tenacity into perspective; they were on their way.

Unable to check into the arranged Birdwing Motel on our arrival, we were soon given keys to our rooms at the Ori Hotel, where I put on a carton of SP for us all, and our team enjoyed our last evening together. The two teachers I was to interview couldn't attend after all, so we simply relaxed, enjoying our SP and taking photographs instead, with Clyde presenting me with a pair of delicately hand-painted wooden earrings that I wore for the evening. I thanked Sam, Grayson and Clyde for the immense privilege of working with them, and we will happily stay in touch sharing our news into the future.

I will miss each and every teacher and colleague in this compelling country, which continues to enchant me as I prepare to leave, the Northern villages and their endearing People now etched into my life, joining the indelible Kokoda Track and Port Moresby's Southeastern Coast.

Two months later, just before Father's Day, Grayson broke the tragic news that Clyde had been murdered in Popondetta, stabbed to death by an assailant who remained undetained. He is survived by his wife and beautiful 3-year-old daughter.

Since this crucial 2019 report was presented to the PNG Government, some teachers who originally received Government training attained their accreditations under KTF's Teach for Tomorrow program before returning to Government payroll.

Others continue their training under a 3 to 4-year Diploma or Bachelor of Primary Teaching, the newly introduced legislation, while a number remain under KTF employment, fulfilling their careers.

KTF remains committed to the future of education in rural PNG, supporting as many of tomorrow's teachers through these educational reforms as resources allow.

* * *

KTF teachers from Kou Kou Infants, Kokoda, Hoi and Alola and Kovelo Elementary and Primary Schools. Kokoda College 2019.

KTF's Kokoda College, Kokoda 2019

KTF teachers from Gorari, Kebara, Waju and Kokoda, Gorari 2019.

KTF teachers Neil (left) from Sanananda and Walter (right) from Buna Elementary Schools, Sanananda 2019.

Sam Kaima (left) and Grayson Kaumi (right) KTF Project Managers.

Clyde Arabata, our driver, Kokoda 2019.

Japanese airstrip, Sanananda 2019

Sanananda Beach 2019

Decaying remains of 1942 Japanese landing barges, Sanananda 2019.

Grandma Charlotte, Sanananda 2019.

Chapter 6

Kokoda Track Foundation's Origins and Programs

> Giving a Little Back

Co-founders of KTF, Dr Genevieve Nelson (CEO) and Patrick Lindsay, journalist/writer and documentarist, Yahoo Serious, actor and film director, and Bill James, co-founder of Flight Centre, established this remarkable operation in 2003.

One mighty ideal; repay our debt to PNG's legendary citizens and countrymen for their commitment to our Australian troops during our desperate months under the threat of Japanese invasion during World War 2.

One powerful agenda; mastermind an educational platform for schools and hospitals to secure a safe future for our struggling island neighbour.

Spearheading the graduation of these remarkable teachers is the Archer Leadership Program designed by KTF to provide these new graduates with a 12-month Australian learning program, mentoring, work experience and an opportunity to experience the Australian lifestyle.

Reciprocally, these outstanding Archer leaders return to PNG with an extended vision to empower their country's future generations.

Twenty extraordinary years later...

By 2023, KTF's *Teach for Tomorrow* project had successfully trained 3,685 dedicated Elementary teachers across 14 remote and rural Papua New Guinea Provinces, delivering quality education and bringing solar lighting to over 136,000 children in these often isolated regions.

KTF's *Teach for Tomorrow II* continues to provide ongoing mentoring, upskilling and training to increasing numbers of these inspirational teachers, often limited to sole-teacher, multigrade schools. These dedicated teachers continue to evolve vital skills under KTF's *Train the Trainer* model in conjunction with provincial education partners.

Arguably, one of KTF'S most influential models is *Teach for Tomorrow, Early Years*, the next series of professional teacher development. A framework for early childhood education, KTF continues working alongside Provincial Departments of Education to develop Early Childhood Education for their province and enable a pathway for elementary teachers to specialise in educating PNG's youngest minds at their most critical development.

Kokoda College's *Flexible Open Distance Education (FODE)* program offers young adults and school leavers the opportunity to continue their high school education, matriculating at Grade 12 level. Others who have studied previously can also upgrade their results to Grade 12 standard, improving their minimum entry requirements into tertiary teaching and health worker courses.

Students committed to training as teachers and health workers are accepted into the FODE program and supported to pursue tertiary studies after graduating from Kokoda College. Presently, a cohort of 184 students undertake their matriculation studies.

The recent years - 2019-2022...

2022

Manari Village now proudly hosts Kokoda College's satellite centre and first high school along the Kokoda Track, *Mt Koiari FODE Centre*. Opened in 2022, KTF brought FODE training to the remote reaches of the Track, eliminating the trainees' arduous overland trek across the Owen Stanley Range to Kokoda College. The centre enrolled 30 students across Grades 9 to 11 in its inaugural year.

2020

2020's introduction to Covid dawned with the opening of the *Motu Koita FODE Centre*, Port Moresby. Located in a building provided by the Motu Koita Assembly Education Infrastructure Project, the Centre is operated by KTF and is nationally recognised by the PNG National FODE office. It offers Grades 9, 10, 11 and 12 studies to local students wanting to upgrade their education to pursue teaching and health careers.

The centre uses a digitised version of the FODE curriculum, and all students are given a tablet to support their studies. Each term, students rotate between face-to-face group lectures, one-on-one tutoring, and self-directed study at home.

2019

Balimo College and satellite centres are a *PNG Sustainable Development Program (SDP)* education initiative managed by KTF.

Commencing operations in 2019, Balimo College rapidly became KTF's largest FODE centre, with 300 students studying Grades 9 to 12. In an exciting development, 2022 saw the College commence the Diploma of Primary Teaching, the first in Western Province to offer the course, with an inaugural cohort of 40 enrolled students.

The demand for studies in rural and remote Western Province led to the establishment of two additional satellite centres in these remote areas; *Morehead FODE Centre* in South Fly and *St Gabriel's FODE Centre*, Kiunga in North Fly.

KTF's 20-year history in colour...

Follow KTF's unique journey narrated by Sharyn Ghidella, KTF's Ambassador and Channel 7 News presenter:
www.ktf.ngo/ourjourney

Donations supporting the Kokoda Track Foundation's ongoing education programs and colleges can be made through:
www.ktf.ngo/donate-2

***

Dr Genevieve Nelson, Co-Founder of Kokoda Track Foundation.
Photograph courtesy of Kokoda Track Foundation.

Chapter 7

Legacies of the Carriers

> Faole Bokoi - as told by his son, Saii
> Faole, Chief of Manari Village

B attle was imminent for Kokoda.
   Bert Kienzle knew war was coming, so he walked the Track warning its vulnerable communities to flee for their lives and take refuge in the jungle's safe havens.

On hearing this, my grandfather, Late Bokoi, warned his children to prepare food and move out off the Track to seek shelter from the Japanese and Australian artillery fire. My grandfather came back to Manari Village to see for himself if his house was still standing.

As he arrived in the village with my dad, Faole Bokoi, who was then a 16-year-old boy, the Australian New Guinea Administration Unit (ANGAU) Officer saw my dad and came directly to him, asking him to lift both his hands up for the ANGAU Officer to check under his armpits; if they could grow hair, then he was fit enough to work for the Australian soldiers carrying food supplies. From this time, my dad was confirmed by the ANGAU Officer and commenced his duty as a War Carrier.

One of his duties was carrying food supplies from Camp 88, situated between Ofi Creek and Myola, dropping off the supplies where the Australians used Myola's open grassland as an airstrip. On one occasion, while returning to Camp 88 and suffering from exhaustion and blisters on his shoulders, he rested for two days in Manari to recover.

His boss called on a radio asking for him in a number of possible locations, and the other ANGAU Officer who received the call responded, saying *Faole is here at Manari*. His boss ordered my dad to walk immediately to Camp 88, so the Manari officer gave him some biscuits and bully beef before sending him away.

My dad left Manari and arrived late afternoon at Camp 88 around 6:00 pm. His elder brothers, Guia Kerea, Tavu Taeta and Sori Io ran to meet him at the same time as the ANGAU Officer asked about my dad. Guia Kerea said *Yes, Boss, Faole has arrived. He's in the camp.*

The officer told Guia to send my dad to him, so Dad walked to the officer to show him the blisters on his shoulders and began explaining himself. The officer was angry with him for wasting two days at Manari and unbuckled his pistol.

Dad knew the officer intended to kill him, so he fled, throwing himself into a dive down the mountain, where a sharp stick gauged a deep wound in his right thigh.

Rolling the entire descent to Ofi Creek, he lay bleeding through the night. His brothers also hid from the officer and searched for my dad through the darkness, thinking that the officer had shot him, having fired his pistol at my dad four times.

My three uncles followed his footprints and blood on the leaves. Angry with the ANGAU Officer, they planned to kill him if my dad died until they finally found him lying on a sandy bank. When Dad saw them, he rose to flee again, but they shouted *It's us looking for you!*

Assured, he lay down again on the sand, and his three brothers ran to him with tears in their eyes, helping him up by the hands to take him to the camp where his wound was dressed by the medic. Dad was told to rest and recover for two weeks until his wound had healed, and then he could continue his duties. His monthly salary was six pounds, ten shillings and five rolls of tobacco for his labour.

When the war ended, Manari Village held the Kokoda Victory celebration with a feast of garden produce and 24 live pigs. At that time, one of the soldiers picked up his rifle and said *What part of the pig do I shoot?,* and the locals shouted *Kinave,* meaning *shoot in the head.*

Kina means *head* in the Koiari language, and the terminology has been perpetually adopted into our national currency, PNG Kina.

My dad felt that he was getting old and his strength fading, so in 2005, he appointed me as Magistrate Chairman to rule eight villages. The sheer lack of government services reaching my ward area led me to my decision to establish a trekking company, which would better enable me to provide financial support to my local communities through the Tourism Industry. This was when my dream was born.

In 2006 I launched my local trekking company, Brigade Hill Tours, partnering with South Sea Horizons in 2007 before leaving Manari in 2008 to successfully fulfil my trekking operations dream.

I am recognised by the local communities as Chief of Manari Village and have worked progressively with the Kokoda Track Foundation (KTF) since 2007.

My career with KTF began in logistics as a volunteer for four years (2007-2010) before extending my role with a two-year contract. In 2013, I became permanently employed as KTF's

Logistics Officer, progressing into my current position as a KTF Project Coordinator, delivering vital community support and hope to the People of the Kokoda Track.

My aim:

Keep the spirit of Kokoda alive.

South Sea Horizons contact details :

Web: https://southseahorizons.com/trips/kokoda-trail/
Email: saii@southseahorizons.com
or   opspng@southseahorizons.com

Late Faole Bokoi (middle of photo) marching on Anzac Day.
Photograph courtesy of Saii Faole.

From left. Late Faole, Late Tavu Taete, Guia Kerea, Eda Bodui, Sori Io in 1996. All were Carriers during World War 2.
Photograph courtesy of Saii Faole.

Late Faole Bokoi (left) and Ginae Bahoe (right).
Photograph courtesy of Saii Faole.

Saii Faole at Bomana War Cemetery, Anzac Day 2019
Photograph courtesy of Saii Faole

> **Raphael Oimbare - Grandfather of Philip Laba, Kokoda Footsteps Trekking**

Raphael Oimbari, my grandfather, was born around 1925 in a small village called Hanau, off the road to Oro Bay near Popondetta. He was a well-disciplined young man, well-active and strong.

When the Kokoda Campaign first arose with the Japanese landings along the Buna-Sanananda Coast, he was recruited as a frontline Carrier of the Fuzzy Wuzzy Angels.

Raphael served as a Carrier from Buna, Sanananda and Oro Bay, escorting and carrying casualties along the Track, including those of the 2/10th Battalion in 1942 and 1943.

Aside from the hard work, the young Raphael Oimbari shared sacrifice, courage, mateship and endurance with the Australian soldiers providing them with comfort, support and assistance in all conditions; the jungle darkness, torrential rain and exhausting, sleepless nights.

My grandfather was spotted on Christmas Day in 1942, escorting the injured Australian soldier, Private George (Dick) Whittington of the 2/10th Battalion, when he was photographed by George Silk along the road to the Aid Station at Buna. This timeless photograph was also published in a New Zealand magazine in 1943 and has become an iconic image worldwide depicting the gentle, humanitarian nature of our famous Fuzzy Wuzzy Angels.

After the war, my grandfather stayed in Hanau Village, collecting war relics and disbursing them among our courageous World War 2 survivors.

In 1993, he received the Order of British Empire (OBE) before sadly passing away in 1996. Raphael Oimbare was given a state funeral upon his death, and his grave can be visited along the road to Hanau Village, Oro Bay.

* * *

Philip Laba has a business mantra; *We retrace the footsteps of our forefathers, the Fuzzy Wuzzy Angels, who struggled in 1942.*

From a young boy attending Laloki Secondary and then Sogeri National High School, Philip knew he was destined to follow in his gallant grandfather's footsteps. Achieving this dream would take sacrifice and study, and his sights were clearly set on completing his business studies at the Institute of Business Studies, Saraga Campus, 6 Mile, PNG.

On graduating, he led a local trekking company as Head Guide until launching his own company, Kokoda Footsteps Trekking, in 2011. Today, the successful business owner and professional guide acknowledges those challenges.

I've been a struggling person in the PNG tourism business. Now, I am blessed with the results of my hard work. It's a cry out for my people of the Kokoda Track.

Committed to providing a better future for these remote communities, Philip recently opened a phonics school at Owers Corner for teaching Years 1 and 2 the intricate skills of English phonics, with 50 children registered and attending classes. His vision carries these young futures on his shoulders, as did Raphael Oimbare's for the wounded of 1942.

Kokoda Footsteps Trekking contact details:
 Kokoda Footsteps Trekking P.O. Box 3102, Boroko NCD
 Mobile: +675 72241 835
 Email: kokodafootsteps@gmail.com
     philiplaba@gmail.com

Raphael Oimbare escorting George (Dick) Whittington near Buna in 1942.
Photograph courtesy of Philip Laba.

Raphael Oimbare (far right) on parade in 1942.
Photograph courtesy of News Dog Media.

Philip Laba, Proprietor of Kokoda Footsteps Trekking and
Raphael Oimbare's grandson, displays a collection of
ammunition relics.
Photograph courtesy of Philip Laba.

Raphael Oimbare (far left) in a procession of Carriers transporting wounded soldiers to a Medical Station near Buna in 1942.
Photograph courtesy of the Australian War Memorial.

Tropymus Suma and George Suma - Grandfather and Bubu Grandfather of Maryanne Suma

My grandfather carried food supplies, but this isn't just *his* brave story.

There were two brothers, my grandfather Tropymus Suma and his younger brother, George, both from Amanda Village, Kokoda, and have since passed away. In PNG culture, a grandfather's younger brother is known as a *bubu* grandfather, not a great uncle, making George Suma my *bubu* grandfather.

My uncle and aunty tell me stories of their very awful and hard labour. Grandfather Tropymus, *Bubu* Grandfather George and other Kokoda men worked together, burying the dead Australian soldiers in a temporary cemetery where the Kokoda Primary School now stands. Later, they were ordered to dig up the bodies for reinterring at Bomana War Cemetery. It was horrific work.

My grandfather and one of his friends escorted an Australian missionary from Milne Bay to safety at Mt Albert, around 70 km North/North West of Kokoda, where its towering metal cross overlooks the ranges. Tropymus visited the famous cross, spending some quiet time at its base before he and his friend commenced their perilous journey home to Amanda Village. Their other companions who began the journey with them had become weak and sick along the way, stopping to set up camp to recover while they waited for their return.

Tropymus was a humble, helpful man with a great and powerful history, which gives me great pride and joy. I am blessed to be his granddaughter, and I thank God the Almighty for my dad and grandfather.

My dad's name is Jimmy Johnsford Suma, and his brother is Eite James Suma. My dad was a soldier in the Pacific Island Regiment Volunteers, A Company, before Papua New Guinea's independence.

* * *

The Suma name remains at the heart of the Kokoda community. Maryanne Suma honours her grandfathers' legacies in her role as an independent and enterprising woman cooking irresistible meals for families, the staff at Kokoda College and sometimes visitors to the Track. The family continues trekking in their grandfathers' footsteps ushering trekkers across the Owen Stanley Range in homage to the Australian soldiers and the heroic Carriers like Tropymus and George Suma.

Their exhausted struggles ensured supplies were delivered to the battle-weary soldiers, their bruised shoulders bore the injured to safety, and those laid to rest were respectfully buried by their gentle, careful hands.

If not for them...

Maryanne Suma and bubu at Kokoda Village.
Photograph courtesy of Maryanne Suma.

Iriap Razi - Grandfather of Sam Geseng

Pre-war, Sam Geseng's 18-year-old grandfather, Iriap Razi, was a Papua New Guinea-born Australian Police Officer of PNG's Light Force, stationed halfway between Buna and Lae in the Northeast Coast village of Dantap, Kaiapit, and Markham District in Morobe Province. When war arrived on his peaceful shores, Iriap immediately engaged in active service carrying cargo for the Australian army, the Australian Military Force (AMF), until recruited into the Royal Papuan Constabulary.

One of eight Carriers captured together in Lae by the Japanese, the group's alliance with the Australians was soon revealed, dooming them to execution at 3:00 pm the next afternoon. Determined to live, Iriap tried to persuade his friends to escape with him, but the fear of being caught twice prevented all except one from agreeing and working together on a plan.

There were few resources until the sticks of sugar cane they chewed suddenly became their life-saving tool to freedom. Each stick of cane they finished chewing was thrown gradually closer to the Namanula Prison Camp's perimeter as the men wandered within the camp, knowing they were being closely watched by the Japanese guards. Their seemingly natural routine brought no suspicion, and they continued to engineer their plan entirely under the guards' vigilant gaze.

Courageously, a final unassuming throw enabled the pair's escape, returning them fleetly to the jungle's sanctuary, with the Japanese pursuing them equally as swiftly. Freedom was only as guaranteed as the two men's ability to rely on their sharply honed survival skills and strategic tactics, training that Iriap relied upon throughout his service and everyday life. Their own skills would now determine life or death.

Hiding beneath a log in the nearby lake with his nose barely above the water to allow him to breathe, Iriap stayed motionless for hours until darkness finally brought the safety of its cover. He was alone. The Japanese who had chased the two men abandoned him to hunt down his friend. Iriap would be the sole survivor.

Finally making his way back to his village in Markham Valley, Morobe Province, he was given food and some fire to warm himself. He began helping others to escape until the Japanese inevitably arrived, identifying Iriap and causing him to flee once again. He continued to help others escape and evade the Japanese, including two men from a neighbouring village behind the mountain. In their gratitude, the two villages would later offer Iriap a gift of two women as his sisters, who accompanied him on his return home when it was safe following the war. They would marry men from Iriap's village and begin families there, with one of the sons taking Iriap's name as his namesake.

Until then, Iriap continued his duties in the Royal Papuan Constabulary, transferring to Bougainville and New Ireland, the northern islands off Lae's beaches, engaging in the defiant ejection of Japan's South Seas Detachment. His dedication to duty would see this disciplined and formidable Papua New Guinean stationed in Bougainville, West and East Sepik, Madang, the Solomons and, substantially, New Ireland Province before returning to Morobe Province in later years with his wife. An outstanding hunter and immensely respected, Iriap took care of everyone in the village, his privileged position establishing him as the first of his People to be paid in Australian dollars by the Australian Government.

* * *

And now, the children of Morobe Province and the Huon Gulf District, the same age as Sam when his grandfather passed away in 1969, studiously uphold Sam's mentoring and scholastic compass as Morobe District Director for Education, his natural leadership following in Iriap's footsteps.

Having completed his high school education through an Australian scholarship in Lae and further university studies, Sam travelled to Australia, the USA and British Columbia under international AVATAR programs empowering his career path.

From a dedicated primary school teacher, Sam progressed through his dedication and hard work to School Inspector under the National Department of Education before attaining the pivotal role of District Education Advisor under the Morobe Provincial Administration. Here, Sam became responsible for implementing government curriculums and education legislation throughout the provinces.

Today, overseeing the education services of Huon Gulf at the beating heart of Iriap Razi's Morobe Province, Sam Geseng guides his 700 dutiful teachers to shape their 25,000 students into tomorrow's leaders.

Iriap Razi (2nd from left, front row) in a group photo of the Royal Papuan Constabulary, Bougainville, February 1944.
Photograph courtesy of Australian War Memorial.

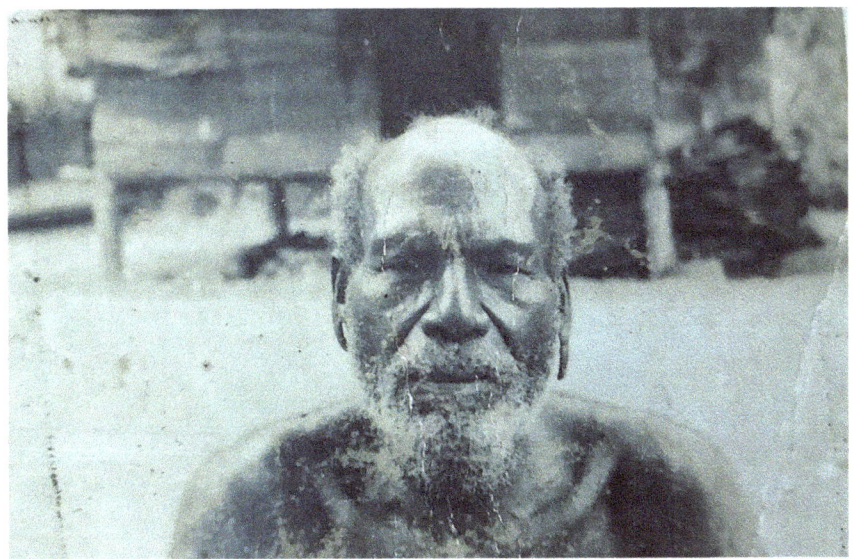

Iriap Razi, veteran of the Royal Papuan Constabulary.
Photograph courtesy of Sam Geseng.

Sam Geseng, Iriap Razi's grandson.
Photograph courtesy of Sam Geseng.

Rampiri - Grandfather of Evelyn Jarua

This is the traditional wartime story of how my grandfathers fought the raiding parties in the aftermath of World War 2 and escaped to safety, as retold by my father Lawrence Jarua. I like to title it *The Magical Spear Fight With the Orokaivans.*

When WWII reached PNG's Northern Province, Oro, most of our village people were still living in their traditional ways with little exposure to the outside world. They had known war in the traditional context of fighting with their enemy tribes using traditional homemade weapons, unlike warplanes, bombs etc. So it was a shocking and frightening experience for them, making them thankful for the early missionaries established there who guided them to safety.

It was the aftermath of WWII in our village called Oere, Higaturu LLG, Sohe District of Oro Province. Some local people started organizing groups pretending to be warlords raiding destroyed villages, and therefore, it remained unsafe for our People to return to Oere Village straight away.

Our clan *Garepa* were hiding in a cave in the forest for safety all throughout the duration of WWII. My grandfather, Rampiri, came to check their gardens to see if it was destroyed or not and also to check if the war had truly ended so he can inform our clan to come back to their village. A few weeks earlier, my grandmother had given birth to my big daddy and worried should anything happen to my grandfather.

Grandfather Rampiri and his elder brother took off to check the gardens and village, regardless, arriving safely at their destroyed village and gardens. After inspecting the damage, they were collecting food crops from their garden when they heard the sounds of engines coming up the nearby road. They were quite curious to see this strange, loud machinery as all these were new to them.

They both hid behind the bushes along the road to watch the vehicle pass, to determine if these were real defence forces or one of the local groups rumoured to be impersonating defence personnel to raid the villages; they weren't soldiers. Unfortunately, one of the raiders in the vehicle spotted them, their discovery resulting in a magical fistfight.

Outnumbered by a group of ten men, they never compromised, ferociously fighting the armed raiders using only their spears. During the battle, they were caught briefly at gunpoint, when without clearly knowing what a gun was, my grandfather pulled the gun from the raider and broke it with his bare hands. In total, they both broke ten guns from the pretend soldiers.

These two men were something else. As an anthropologist, I define them as no ordinary people; they were warriors of *Garepa Clan*, well-trained to defend themselves and protect their land from intruders.

After breaking the guns and injuring the fake soldiers, my grandfathers escaped into the bush, informing their clan members of the incidents and declaring it unsafe to return to their village. Until then, they would remain secluded.

When news of the fake soldiers spread, Chiefs from nearby villages came out strongly and threatened the group to end their village raids so their people can return to their village once again. They called for peace in a traditional way. Clan warriors were tasked to perform continuous assessments of situations until it was safe for women and children to return to their villages after WWII ended.

My grandfathers were the last living giants in the Orokaiva society. In fact, our clan *Garepa* is the name of *giants*, so I basically come from a clan with a long history of giant warriors. My grandfather had long raster hair and wore what is called *Malo,* a cloth called tapa cloth, made from the bark of a tree, to cover the private parts. He wore armlets, a headdress and a sling bag across his chest. By tradition, tattoos adorned his face and arms, legs and back, and he carried his spear as if it were a part of him.

My father says his raster hair was so long and thick that he used it to cover himself during cold, wet weather hunting trips. His armlets, which we still have today, can fit an ordinary man's thigh but not his arm; he was a powerful and big man.

* * *

Over eight decades since Rampiri and his brother's fight with the village raiders, Evelyn carries the fire of her grandfather's spirit into the future as the first female from her father's village to attain a Bachelor of Arts Degree, achieving double majors in Social Works and Anthropology. Her natural leadership empowers others to use education as a pathway to bring change, especially women and youths.

Graduating from the University of Papua New Guinea in 2017, Evelyn joined the Justice Department, Port Moresby, where she implemented the S2SC Program for child safety in schools. This important program supports the valuable work of PNG Kids Australia, where Evelyn volunteers to supply reading materials to remote schools throughout numerous provinces.

Attaining her Anthropology Degree has amplified Evelyn's important connection with her People and their customs. With PNG's traditional stories and cultural history verbally passed down through their Knowledge Keepers, the modern generations have disconnected from tradition and as a result, precious knowledge is tragically lost before being recorded. To protect these lost treasures, Evelyn created a blog on WordPress called *Dasiro* and a Facebook page *Dasiro Photography* where she shares lost traditional history and stories for posterity.

Evelyn's warrior spirit continues Rampiri's legacy to sustain her People's traditions and culture into an uncertain future.

Evelyn Jarua, granddaughter of Rampiri.
Photograph courtesy of Evelyn Jarua.

> **Adifuekava Magaidimo - Grandfather of Jansen Nesai (Jaywoods Tours)**

Jansen Nesai's grandfather, Adifuekava Magaidimo, would not speak of the difficulties experienced during those torrid years. Like countless others subjected to the irreversible visions of war, Magaidimo remained silent under the weight of his painful memories, the familiar, age-old retreat of veterans worldwide. Peace and family led the way.

Now, 80 years later, studding the crystal waters surrounding Alotau and the Trobriand Islands lie the decaying reminders of the war-torn era that belonged to the resolute Carrier's generation. These remnants now capture the imagination of today's foreign visitors, particularly Australians.

Jansen continues his family-operated tour company, Jaywoods Tours, providing tourists from all countries with bus tours around Milne Bay's villages and historical World War 2 sites, as well as boat charters out to some of the stunning islands dotted along the coast. Cruise passengers booking Jaywood's day trips to Papua New Guinea's jewel of destinations receive VIP hospitality as welcomed guests and are treated to generations of local knowledge.

Jaywoods Tours Contact details:
    Facebook: www.facebook.com/people/Jaywoods-TOURS
    Email: jansenjayvannesai@gmail.com
    Mobile: +675 7341 5984

* * *

> ### Kenda Suma - Grandfather of Chris Suma (PNGLET Trekking)

Chris Suma's grandfather, Kenda Suma, was a Carrier along the Kokoda Track during World War 2, and his story begins quite differently from others. Historically, Chris' grandparents were the first to meet the earliest white man in Kokoda when their quiet Amanda Village consisted of only five houses. The Census was held following this iconic meeting.

Today, Chris honours his grandfather's courage by caring for visiting trekkers making the formidable journey across the Owen Stanley Range, just as the Australian troops did over 80 years ago in a brutal, bloody world that was Papua New Guinea under invasion.

No longer do the mountains crackle with the staccato of Bren Guns or resonate to the billowing echo of army-issue .303 rifles, though. Instead, Chris' trekkers raise their cold, rain-soaked faces to the sound of encroaching thunder reverberating through valleys, a reminder of the ruthless terrain they have entered and how far they remain at its mercy until they reach the comfort of their waiting dry shelter.

And with every step, Chris and his porters are vigilant. Every move is sensed. Every sound alerting. This is his nature, as was his Grandfather Kenda's. Chris does his memory proud, and Kenda's spirit lives on.

PNGLET Trekking contact details:
- Email: pnglet.trekking@gmail.com or chrisesuma08@gmail.com
- Mobile: +675 79007754 (Digicel/WhatsApp) or +675 78939520 (Telekom)
- Facebook: PNGLET Trekking

> **Benedict Sawa - Father of George Malasi (Bougainville Tourism Consult.)**

George Malasi's grandfather, Benedict Sawa, was obliged to help the Japanese cooks in the Bougainville reaches of Papua New Guinea. The father of George's mother, Benedict was a *Kukurai* with the Australian Colonial Government, a role which would later become the equivalent of a 1970s Patrol Officer.

After extensive fighting along an increasing North Eastern front in 1944, the Allies captured the Japanese-occupied Nissan Green Island, its lagoon primarily a sea-plane base for Japanese Navy H6K Mavis Flying Boats and F1M2 Pete Floatplanes, Nissan Green Island was finally flying the Australian flag. Allied landing craft swiftly arrived on the island's oil-stained beaches, delivering heavy equipment for building roads that were soon crisscrossing the island's jungle heart.

A lifetime on, George brings tourism to peaceful Nissan Green Island in the Autonomous Region of Bougainville, his home and eastern gem in the crown of PNG's coastline.

Bougainville Tourism Consultancies contact details:
   Email: bougtourismconsultancies@gmail.com.
   Phone number: +675 73490479

* * *

Simon Tourita - Grandfather of Jay Why Tee

My grandfather was what we call a *Luluai* in the village, the *Peacemaker*. As a hunter, he had a pack of dogs led by their dog leader, *Boroilam*, meaning *pig hunter*.

I was very young when he passed, around three years old. During his traditional funeral, I remember holding my dad's hand as we walked with what we call *Tubuans*, a part of our sacred Tolai society for men only. This is one of the occasions when *Tubuans* come out after an important figure in the village passes away, and shell money is broken.

All PNG provinces have their own individual types of shell money called *tabu*, which is made of tiny seashells put together by canes.

* * *

Separated by 600 km of the South Pacific Ocean from his grandfather's traditional home of Rabaul, Jay Why Tee's broadcasts celebrate that same peace and freedom to Port Moresby's population as PNG's Legend FM radio announcer.

Like his grandfather, Jay Why Tee brings his own unique presence to the attentive masses, the new generation of a captivated audience.

> **James Koeba Obara - Uncle of David Obara**

David Obara's uncle, James, was also a Carrier who remained silent, shouldering his memories alone.

Today, David is a principal landowner who has built a primary school for the 1,600 occupants of his Yule Island community, 160 km North West of Port Moresby.

This crucial achievement was only made possible by his uncle's courage and commitment, one of many among Papua New Guinea's finest warriors.

* * *

Yule Island, New Guinea, May 1944. Members of the Royal Papuan Constabulary on parade, ANGAU, Kairuka Station.
Photograph courtesy of Australian War Memorial

Yule Island, New Guinea, May 1944. Staff Sergeant Robinson, ANGAU HQ, with native customers waiting outside the trading store on Kairuka Station.
Photograph courtesy of Australian War Memorial.

Grandfather of Willie Hindom

Willie Hindom's grandfather was a Police Officer of the Dutch Niugini Government in Irian Jaya, now known as Western Papua, when the Japanese invaded Dutch Niugini in March 1942.

His grandparents later arrived in PNG in 1960 before Indonesia took over the formerly known Irian Jaya (West Papua) in early 1960 when most West Papuans moved across to Papua New Guinea. It was here where Willie's mother & her siblings grew up.

Willie, his siblings & cousins were born later, growing up in PNG until his father, Matthew Mayer, a Church Parishioner, relocated Willie's immediate family temporarily to Redcliffe, Queensland, where they attended school until returning to their beloved country in the 1980s.

Almost prophetically, his grandfather's vision enables Willie and his family to live freely while West Papua continues its unwavering campaign for independence under Indonesia's staunch control.

* * *

Somewhere Along the Kokoda Track

The Kokoda Track winds onwards through its secrets in the dark,
While the beauty of the jungle drenched in moonlight breaks your heart.
And the Bird of Paradise in the canopy won't reveal itself to you,
But that's not what our Boys were here for back in 1942.

They were called to protect our countries in terrain they'd never seen,
Led by men brave and courageous but High Command was downright mean.
Their bodies were wracked with injuries, exhaustion and disease,
But against all odds they fought all this and the blooded Japanese.

Forward and back and forward again they retook the airfield at Kokoda,
Then pushed them back into the sea from Buna to Salamaua.
The lifeline though along the Track for the Diggers maimed and mangled
Was each stretcher-bearing shoulder of the Fuzzy Wuzzy Angels.

The Porters now are descendants of the Fuzzy Wuzzies from the day,
And are as kind and ever watchful keeping their trekkers from harm's way,
For they will put themselves at risk to ensure you are safe yourself,
And without a sound they'll grab you before you slip off that muddy shelf.

The guns are rusting relics now and the jungle's reclaimed its own,
While the torrential rains and thunderstorms bring a quiet you've never known.
And you sit in quiet reverie in the shadow of their fate,
Ever contemplating the horror of our Boys' muddy, bloody state.

Now the mountains beckon silently beyond the fallen in their graves,
And the trekkers pay their homage in the footsteps of the brave.
For it's a place to fulfil a lifelong dream and feel your spirit change,
Somewhere along the Kokoda Track in the Owen Stanley Range.

To those who belong to the Kokoda Track.......then and now.

Ruth James

About the Author

Ruth James - Allied Learning
(alliedlearningonline@gmail.com)
Photograph courtesy of Clyde Arabata.

As a *TESOL* English teacher, Ruth's inherent passion for writing and history includes her internationally published poetry and evolving World War 1 *Legacy's Gate* series.

The accomplished author of *Returned With a Creed*, the World War 1 military history of her grandfather's AIF 9/41st Battalion, Ruth continues his legacy in her novel, *Coming Home From France*, due for release in late 2023.

A twice Queensland Champion shooter from Redcliffe, Ruth has lived in Bundaberg with her family since 1987.

Afterword

Muffled booms announce the darkening afternoon storm that has been building in the updrafts of Summer's sweltering humidity for the past 2 hours. A physical memory descends upon you and tricks the senses into imagining you are there, 2,000 km away on that perilous mountain track.

Just as transporting are the echoes of singing, long vanished yet heralding the grey dawn as you wake; children's laughter as they play on a vine swing; and eager students bustling to be the first to answer, all draw you back to a place etched in your heart.

Reaching to switch on the cordless kettle involuntarily brings stinging tears, and you stand there picturing faraway friends presently lighting fires for *their* morning coffees, rekindling that dream just as surely as the thunder rumbles through the Owen Stanleys.

Visualising life for teachers commissioned in these isolated villages looks as restricted as it sounds, maximising infrequent and limited resources taken largely for granted in more affluent countries. Intermittent deliveries from KTF, Ministry of Education, Books 4 Png Kids, Bilum Books, Trek 4 Education and similar providers are often constricted by funding and availability. Teachers are sometimes assisted by trekkers and family members or friends visiting from the bigger cities, providing general stationery and, occasionally, equipment.

Nature, too, intervenes with cyclones and monsoonal flooding resulting in closed roads, cancelled chopper deliveries and the prevalent risk of devastating earthquakes requiring long-term recoveries. Seemingly, they can't win a trick, but to witness their determination and drive is inspirational, nonetheless. Their imagination knows no bounds.

As an educational platform, Allied Learning's online deliveries are often impacted by PNG's Digicel technology or limited phone credit, with lessons entirely dependent on video links through phones. Undeterred, persisting with emailed activities has proven to be a practical alternative wherever possible, enabling teachers to at least draw the exercises on their black/white boards where printers are not available. KTF has been a wonderful backstop for printing and delivering these activities, although lack of funding ultimately remains an ever continuing issue.

Their individual missions reflect how these remarkable teachers dig deep to deliver the future to their blossoming students, and in time, these same students offer themselves and their hopes to PNG's future.

It is my entrenched hope to return to these cheery classrooms once again from Port Moresby to Lae when commitments permit, continuing the 2013 dream that led me here.

* * *

Acknowledgements

My express thanks to my family and brother Cliff, dear friend Saii Faole and those continuing this passionate journey, particularly Dr Genevieve Nelson and the Kokoda Track Foundation team. You made this dream possible. My further sincere thanks go to all listed below and anyone accidentally overlooked:

The Australian War Memorial
Anzac Day Commemoration Committee
South Sea Horizons and 2013/2015 trekkers
Barnabas Omi and his team of professional porters.
Efogi Primary School - Mr W. Lovai and students.
Edevu Primary School - Mr M. Barnabas, Tau Maleva,
Bernadine Kilalang, all teachers and students.
Philip Laba - Kokoda Footsteps Trekking
Maryanne Suma
Sam Geseng
Evelyn Jarua
Jansen Nesai - Jaywoods Tours
Chris Suma - PNGLET Trekking
George Malasi - Bougainville Tourism Consultancies
Jay Why Tee - Broadcaster of Legend FM, PNG.
David Obara
Willie Hindom
Victor Kirkwood and Kathy Blundstone
The Stedman Family and Pru Pegg
Sandy Munro and Kelly Gatt
Garricks Camera House, Bundaberg.
Pacific Wrecks
Aviation Safety Network

Farewell

Port Moresby 2015.

www.ingramcontent.com/pod-product-compliance
Lightning Source LLC
Chambersburg PA
CBHW051536010526
44107CB00064B/2749